Praise for Cl___ _g

"In the journey to all things Agile, Uncle Bob has been there, done that, and has both the t-shirt and the scars to show for it. This delightful book is part history, part personal stories, and all wisdom. If you want to understand what Agile is and how it came to be, this is the book for you."

—Grady Booch

"Bob's frustration colors every sentence of *Clean Agile*, but it's a justified frustration. What *is* in the world of Agile development is nothing compared to what *could be*. This book is Bob's perspective on what to focus on to get to that 'what could be.' And he's been there, so it's worth listening."

—Kent Beck

"It's good to read Uncle Bob's take on Agile. Whether just beginning, or a seasoned *agilista*, you would do well to read this book. I agree with almost all of it. It's just some of the parts make me realize my own shortcomings, darn it. It made me double-check our code coverage (85.09%)."

—Jon Kern

"This book provides a historical lens through which to view Agile development more fully and accurately. Uncle Bob is one of the smartest people I know, and he has boundless enthusiasm for programming. If anyone can demystify Agile development, it's him."

—From the Foreword by Jerry Fitzpatrick

Clean Agile

Robert C. Martin Series

Visit **informit.com/martinseries** for a complete list of available publications.

The Robert C. Martin Series is directed at software developers, team-leaders, business analysts, and managers who want to increase their skills and proficiency to the level of a Master Craftsman.

Clean Code presents the principles, patterns, and practices of writing clean code and challenges programmers to closely read code, discovering what's right and what's wrong with it.

Clean Coder provides practical guidance on how to approach software development and work well and clean with a software team.

Clean Craftsmanship picks up where *Clean Code* leaves off, outlining additional ways to write quality and trusted code you can be proud of every day.

Clean Agile is a clear and concise guide to basic Agile values and principles. Perfect for those new to Agile methods and long-time developers who want to simplify approaches for the better.

Clean Architecture brings the methods and tactics of "clean coding" to system design.

Pearson

twitter.com/informIT

informIT.com
the trusted technology learning source

Clean Agile

BACK TO BASICS

Robert C. Martin

♦♦Addison-Wesley

Boston • Columbus • New York • San Francisco • Amsterdam • Cape Town
Dubai • London • Madrid • Milan • Munich • Paris • Montreal • Toronto • Delhi
Mexico City • São Paulo • Sydney • Hong Kong • Seoul • Singapore • Taipei • Tokyo

For information about buying this title in bulk quantities, or for special sales opportunities (which may include electronic versions; custom cover designs; and content particular to your business, training goals, marketing focus, or branding interests), please contact our corporate sales department at corpsales@pearsoned.com or (800) 382-3419.

For government sales inquiries, please contact governmentsales@pearsoned.com.

For questions about sales outside the U.S., please contact intlcs@pearson.com.

Visit us on the Web: informit.com

Library of Congress Control Number: 2019945397

Copyright © 2020 Pearson Education, Inc.

Cover image: Peresanz/Shutterstock

Foreword by Jerry Fitzpatrick, Software Renovation Corporation, March 2019. Used with permission.

Chapter 7 by Sandro Mancuso, April 27, 2019. Used with permission.

Afterword by Eric Crichlow, April 5, 2019. Used with permission.

ISBN-13: 978-0-13-578186-9
ISBN-10: 0-13-578186-8

ScoutAutomatedPrintLine

To every programmer who ever tilted at windmills or waterfalls.

CONTENTS

FOREWORD

What exactly is Agile development? How did it originate? How has it evolved?

In this book, Uncle Bob provides thoughtful answers to these questions. He also identifies the many ways in which Agile development has been misinterpreted or corrupted. His perspective is relevant because he is an authority on the subject, having participated in the birth of Agile development.

Bob and I have been friends for many years. We first met when I joined the telecommunications division of Teradyne in 1979. As an electrical engineer, I helped install and support products; later, I became a hardware designer.

About a year after I joined, the company began seeking new product ideas. In 1981, Bob and I proposed an electronic telephone receptionist—essentially a voicemail system with call-routing features. The company liked the concept, and we soon began developing "E.R.—The Electronic Receptionist." Our prototype was state of the art. It ran the MP/M operating system on an Intel 8086 processor. Voice messages were stored on a five-megabyte Seagate ST-506 hard disk. I designed the voice port hardware while Bob started writing the application. When I finished my design, I wrote application code, too, and I have been a developer ever since.

Around 1985 or 1986, Teradyne abruptly halted E.R. development and, unknown to us, withdrew the patent application. It was a business decision that the company would soon regret, and one that still haunts Bob and me.

Eventually, each of us left Teradyne for other opportunities. Bob started a consulting business in the Chicago area. I became a software contractor and instructor. We managed to stay in touch even though I moved to another state.

By the year 2000, I was teaching Object-Oriented Analysis and Design for Learning Tree International. The course incorporated UML and the Unified Software Development Process (USDP). I was well versed in these technologies, but not with Scrum, Extreme Programming, or similar methodologies.

In February 2001, the Agile Manifesto was published. Like many developers, my initial reaction was "The Agile what?" The only manifesto I knew of was from Karl Marx, an avid Communist. Was this Agile thing a call to arms? Dang software radicals!

The Manifesto did start a rebellion of sorts. It was meant to inspire the development of lean, clean code by using a collaborative, adaptive, feedback-driven approach. It offered an alternative to "heavyweight" processes like Waterfall and the USDP.

It has been 18 years since the Agile Manifesto was published. It is, therefore, ancient history to most of today's developers. For this reason, your understanding of Agile development may not line up with the intent of its creators.

This book aims to set the record straight. It provides a historical lens through which to view Agile development more fully and accurately. Uncle Bob is one of the smartest people I know, and he has boundless enthusiasm for programming. If anyone can demystify Agile development, it's him.

—Jerry Fitzpatrick
Software Renovation Corporation
March 2019

PREFACE

This book is not a work of research. I have not done a diligent literature review. What you are about to read are my personal recollections, observations, and opinions about my 20-year involvement with Agile— nothing more, nothing less.

The writing style is conversational and colloquial. My word choices are sometimes a bit crude. And though I am not one to swear, one [slightly modified] curse word made it into these pages because I could think of no better way to convey the intended meaning.

Oh, this book isn't a complete rave. When it struck me as necessary, I cited some references for you to follow. I checked some of my facts against those of other folks who've been in the Agile community as long as I have. I've even asked several folks to provide supplemental and disagreeing points of view in their own chapters and sections. Still, you should not think of this book as a scholarly work. It may be better to think of it as a memoir—the grumblings of a curmudgeon telling all those new-fangled Agile kids to get off his lawn.

This book is for programmers and non-programmers alike. It is not technical. There is no code. It is meant to provide an overview of the original intent of Agile software development without getting into any deep technical details of programming, testing, and managing.

This is a small book. That's because the topic isn't very big. Agile is a small idea about the small problem of small programming teams doing small things. Agile is *not* a big idea about the big problem of big programming teams doing big things. It's somewhat ironic that this small solution to a small problem has a name. After all, the small problem in question was solved in the 1950s and '60s, almost as soon as software was invented. Back in those days, small software teams learned to do small things rather well. However, it all got derailed in the 1970s when the small software teams doing small things got all tangled up in an ideology that thought it should be doing big things with big teams.

Aren't we supposed to be doing big things with big teams? Heavens, no! Big things don't get done by big teams; big things get done by the collaboration of many small teams doing many small things. This is what the programmers in the 1950s and '60s knew instinctively. And it was this that was forgotten in the 1970s.

Why was this forgotten? I suspect it was because of a discontinuity. The number of programmers in the world began to explode in the 1970s. Prior to that, there were only a few thousand programmers in the world. After that, there were hundreds of thousands. Now that number is approaching one hundred million.

Those first programmers back in the 1950s and '60s were not youngsters. They started programming in their 30s, 40s, and 50s. By the 1970s, just when the population of programmers was staring to explode, those oldsters were starting to retire. So the necessary training never occurred. An impossibly young cohort of 20-somethings entered the workforce just as the experienced folks were leaving, and their experience was not effectively transferred.

Some would say that this event started a kind of dark ages in programming. For 30 years, we struggled with the idea that we should be doing big things with big teams, never knowing that the secret was to do many small things with many small teams.

Then in the mid '90s, we began to realize what we had lost. The idea of small teams began to germinate and grow. The idea spread through the community of software developers, gathering steam. In 2000, we realized we needed an industry-wide reboot. We needed to be reminded of what our forebears instinctively knew. We needed, once again, to realize that big things are done by many collaborating small teams doing small things.

To help popularize this, we gave the idea a name. We called it "Agile."

I wrote this preface in the first days of 2019. It's been nearly two decades since the reboot of 2000, and it seems to me that it's time for yet another. Why? Because the simple and small message of Agile has become muddled over the intervening years. It's been mixed with the concepts of Lean,

Kanban, LeSS, SAFe, Modern, Skilled, and so many others. These other ideas are not bad, but they are not the original Agile message.

So it's time, once again, for us to be reminded of what our forebears knew in the '50s and '60s, and what we relearned in 2000. It's time to remember what Agile really is.

In this book, you will find nothing particularly new, nothing astounding or startling, nothing revolutionary that breaks the mold. What you will find is a restatement of Agile as it was told in 2000. Oh, it's told from a different perspective, and we have learned a few things over the last 20 years that I'll include. But overall, the message of this book is the message of 2001 and the message of 1950.

It's an old message. It's a true message. It's a message that gives us the small solution to the small problem of small software teams doing small things.

Register your copy of *Clean Agile* on the InformIT site for convenient access to updates and/or corrections as they become available. To start the registration process, go to informit.com/register and log in or create an account. Enter the product ISBN (9780135781869) and click Submit. Look on the Registered Products tab for an Access Bonus Content link next to this product, and follow that link to access any available bonus materials. If you would like to be notified of exclusive offers on new editions and updates, please check the box to receive email from us.

ACKNOWLEDGMENTS

My first acknowledgment goes to a pair of intrepid programmers who joyously discovered (or rediscovered) the practices contained herein: Ward Cunningham and Kent Beck.

Next in line is Martin Fowler, without whose steadying hand, in those earliest of days, the Agile revolution would likely have been stillborn.

Ken Schwaber deserves a special mention for the indomitable energy he applied toward the promotion and adoption of Agile.

Mary Poppendieck also deserves special mention for the selfless and inexhaustible energy she put into the Agile movement and her shepherding of the Agile Alliance.

In my view, Ron Jeffries, through his talks, articles, blogs, and the persistent warmth of his character, acted as the conscience of the early Agile movement.

Mike Beedle fought the good fight for Agile but was senselessly murdered by a homeless person on the streets of Chicago.

The other original authors of the Agile Manifesto take a special place here:

Arie van Bennekum, Alistair Cockburn, James Grenning, Jim Highsmith, Andrew Hunt, Jon Kern, Brian Marick, Steve Mellor, Jeff Sutherland, and Dave Thomas.

Jim Newkirk, my friend and business partner at the time, worked tirelessly in support of Agile while enduring personal headwinds that most of us (and certainly I) can't begin to imagine.

Next, I'd like to mention the folks who worked at Object Mentor Inc. They all took the initial risk of adopting and promoting Agile. Many of them are in the following photo, taken at the kickoff of the first XP Immersion course.

Back Row: Ron Jeffries, author, Brian Button, Lowell Lindstrom, Kent Beck, Micah Martin, Angelique Martin, Susan Rosso, James Grenning.
Front Row: David Farber, Eric Meade, Mike Hill, Chris Biegay, Alan Francis, Jennifer Kohnke, Talisha Jefferson, Pascal Roy.
Not pictured: Tim Ottinger, Jeff Langr, Bob Koss, Jim Newkirk, Michael Feathers, Dean Wampler, and David Chelimsky.

I'd also like to acknowledge the folks who gathered to form the Agile Alliance. Some of them are in the picture that follows, which was taken at the kickoff meeting of that now-august alliance.

Left to right: Mary Poppendieck, Ken Schwaber, author, Mike Beedle, Jim Highsmith. (Not pictured: Ron Crocker.)

Finally, thanks to all the folks at Pearson, especially my publisher Julie Phifer.

ABOUT THE AUTHOR

Robert C. Martin (Uncle Bob) has been a programmer since 1970. He is co-founder of cleancoders.com, offering on-line video training for software developers, and founder of Uncle Bob Consulting LLC, offering software consulting, training, and skill development services to major corporations worldwide. He served as the Master Craftsman at 8th Light Inc., a Chicago-based software consulting firm.

Mr. Martin has published dozens of articles in various trade journals and is a regular speaker at international conferences and trade shows. He is also the creator of the acclaimed educational video series at cleancoders.com. Mr. Martin has authored and edited many books including the following:

Designing Object-Oriented C++ Applications Using the Booch Method
Patterns Languages of Program Design 3

More C++ Gems

Extreme Programming in Practice

Agile Software Development: Principles, Patterns, and Practices

UML for Java Programmers

Clean Code

The Clean Coder

Clean Architecture

Clean Agile

A leader in the industry of software development, Mr. Martin served three years as the editor-in-chief of the *C++ Report*, and he served as the first chairman of the Agile Alliance.

INTRODUCTION TO AGILE

In February 2001, a group of 17 software experts gathered in Snowbird, Utah, to talk over the deplorable state of software development. At that time, most software was created using ineffective, heavyweight, high-ritual processes like Waterfall and overstuffed instances of the Rational Unified Process (RUP). The goal of these 17 experts was to create a manifesto that introduced a more effective, lighter-weight, approach.

This was no mean feat. The 17 were people of varied experience and strong divergent opinions. Expecting such a group to come to consensus was a long shot. And yet, against all odds, consensus was reached, the Agile Manifesto was written, and one of the most potent and long-lived movements in the software field was born.

Movements in software follow a predictable path. At first there is a minority of enthusiastic supporters, another minority of enthusiastic detractors, and a vast majority of those who don't care. Many movements die in, or at least never leave, that phase. Think of aspect-oriented programming, or logic programming, or CRC cards. Some, however, cross the chasm and become extraordinarily popular and controversial. Some even manage to leave the controversy behind and simply become part of the mainstream body of thought. Object Orientation (OO) is an example of the latter. And so is Agile.

Unfortunately, once a movement becomes popular, the name of that movement gets blurred through misunderstanding and usurpation. Products and methods having nothing to do with the actual movement will borrow the name to cash in on the name's popularity and significance. And so it has been with Agile.

The purpose of this book, written nearly two decades after the Snowbird event, is to set the record straight. This book is an attempt to be as pragmatic as possible, describing Agile without nonsense and in no uncertain terms.

Presented here are the fundamentals of Agile. Many have embellished and extended these ideas—and there is nothing wrong with that. However, those extensions and embellishments are not Agile. They are Agile plus something else. What you will read here is what Agile is, what Agile was, and what Agile will inevitably always be.

HISTORY OF AGILE

When did Agile begin? Probably more than 50,000 years ago when humans first decided to collaborate on a common goal. The idea of choosing small intermediate goals and measuring the progress after each is just too intuitive, and too human, to be considered any kind of a revolution.

When did Agile begin in modern industry? It's hard to say. I imagine the first steam engine, the first mill, the first internal combustion engine, and the first airplane were produced by techniques that we would now call Agile. The reason for that is that taking small measured steps is just too natural and human for it to have happened any other way.

So when did Agile begin in software? I wish I could have been a fly on the wall when Alan Turing was writing his 1936 paper.[1] My guess is that the many "programs" he wrote in that book were developed in small steps with plenty of desk checking. I also imagine that the first code he wrote for the Automatic Computing Engine, in 1946, was written in small steps, with lots of desk checking, and even some real testing.

The early days of software are loaded with examples of behavior that we would now describe as Agile. For example, the programmers who wrote the control software for the Mercury space capsule worked in half-day steps that were punctuated by unit tests.

Much has been written elsewhere about this period. Craig Larman and Vic Basili wrote a history that is summarized on Ward Cunningham's wiki,[2] and also in Larman's book, *Agile & Iterative Development: A Manager's Guide.*[3]

---

1. Turing, A. M. 1936. On computable numbers, with an application to the Entscheidungsproblem [proof]. *Proceedings of the London Mathematical Society, 2* (published 1937), 42(1):230–65. The best way to understand this paper is to read Charles Petzold's masterpiece: Petzold, C. 2008. *The Annotated Turing: A Guided Tour through Alan Turing's Historic Paper on Computability and the Turing Machine.* Indianapolis, IN: Wiley.
2. Ward's wiki, c2.com, is the original wiki—the first ever to have appeared in the internet. Long may it be served.
3. Larman, C. 2004. *Agile & Iterative Development: A Manager's Guide.* Boston, MA: Addison-Wesley.

But Agile was not the only game in town. Indeed, there was a competing methodology that had enjoyed considerable success in manufacturing and industry at large: Scientific Management.

Scientific Management is a top-down, command-and-control approach. Managers use scientific techniques to ascertain the best procedures for accomplishing a goal and then direct all subordinates to follow their plan to the letter. In other words, there is big up-front planning followed by careful detailed implementation.

Scientific Management is probably as old as the pyramids, Stonehenge, or any of the other great works of ancient times, because it is impossible to believe that such works could have been created without it. Again, the idea of repeating a successful process is just too intuitive, and human, to be considered some kind of a revolution.

Scientific Management got its name from the works of Frederick Winslow Taylor in the 1880s. Taylor formalized and commercialized the approach and made his fortune as a management consultant. The technique was wildly successful and led to massive increases in efficiency and productivity during the decades that followed.

And so it was that in 1970 the software world was at the crossroads of these two opposing techniques. Pre-Agile (Agile before it was called "Agile") took short reactive steps that were measured and refined in order to stagger, in a directed random walk, toward a good outcome. Scientific Management deferred action until a thorough analysis and a resulting detailed plan had been created. Pre-Agile worked well for projects that enjoyed a low cost of change and solved partially defined problems with informally specified goals. Scientific Management worked best for projects that suffered a high cost of change and solved very well-defined problems with extremely specific goals.

The question was, what kinds of projects were software projects? Were they high cost of change and well defined with specific goals, or were they low cost of change and partially defined with informal goals?

Don't read too much into that last paragraph. Nobody, to my knowledge, actually asked that question. Ironically, the path we chose in the 1970s appears to have been driven more by accident than intent.

In 1970, Winston Royce wrote a paper[4] that described his ideas for managing large-scale software projects. The paper contained a diagram (Figure 1.1) that depicted his plan. Royce was not the originator of this diagram, nor was he advocating it as a plan. Indeed, the diagram was set up as a straw man for him to knock down in the subsequent pages of his paper.

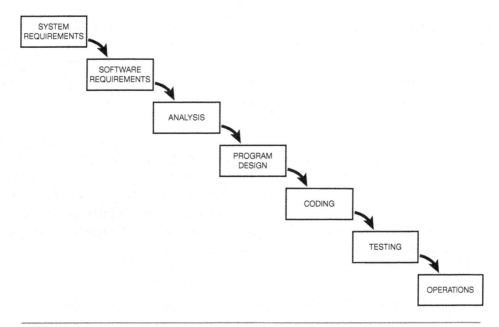

Figure 1.1 Winston Royce's diagram that inspired Waterfall development

Nevertheless, the prominent placing of the diagram, and the tendency for people to infer the content of a paper from the diagram on the first or second page, led to a dramatic shift in the software industry.

---

4. Royce, W. W. 1970. Managing the development of large software systems. *Proceedings, IEEE WESCON,* August: 1–9. Accessed at http://www-scf.usc.edu/~csci201/lectures/Lecture11/royce1970.pdf.

Royce's initial diagram looked so much like water flowing down a series of rocks, that the technique became known as "Waterfall."

Waterfall was the logical descendant of Scientific Management. It was all about doing a thorough analysis, making a detailed plan, and then executing that plan to completion.

Even though it was not what Royce was recommending, it was the concept people took away from his paper. And it dominated the next three decades.[5]

This is where I come into the story. In 1970, I was 18 years old, working as a programmer at a company named A. S. C. Tabulating in Lake Bluff, Illinois. The company had an IBM 360/30 with 16K of core, an IBM 360/40 with 64K of core, and a Varian 620/f minicomputer with 64K of core. I programmed the 360s in COBOL, PL/1, Fortran, and assembler. I wrote only assembler for the 620/f.

It's important to remember what it was like being a programmer back in those days. We wrote our code on coding forms using pencils, and we had keypunch operators punch them onto cards for us. We submitted our carefully checked cards to computer operators who ran our compiles and tests during the third shift because the computers were too busy during the day doing real work. It often took days to get from the initial writing to the first compile, and each turnaround thereafter was usually one day.

The 620/f was a bit different for me. That machine was dedicated to our team, so we had 24/7 access to it. We could get two, three, perhaps even four turnarounds and tests per day. The team I was on was also composed of people who, unlike most programmers of the day, could type. So we would punch our own decks of cards rather than surrendering them to the vagaries of the keypunch operators.

---

5. It should be noted that my interpretation of this timeline has been challenged in Chapter 7 of Bossavit, L. 2012. *The Leprechauns of Software Engineering: How Folklore Turns into Fact and What to Do About It*. Leanpub.

What process did we use during those days? It certainly wasn't Waterfall. We had no concept of following detailed plans. We just hacked away on a day-to-day basis, running compiles, testing our code, and fixing bugs. It was an endless loop that had no structure. It also wasn't Agile, or even Pre-Agile. There was no discipline in the way we worked. There was no suite of tests and no measured time intervals. It was just code and fix, code and fix, day after day, month after month.

I first read about Waterfall in a trade journal sometime around 1972. It seemed like a godsend to me. Could it really be that we could analyze the problem up front, then design a solution to that problem, and then implement that design? Could we really develop a schedule based on those three phases? When we were done with analysis, would we really be one-third done with the project? I felt the power of the concept. I wanted to believe it. Because, if it worked, it was a dream come true.

Apparently I wasn't alone, because many other programmers and programming shops caught the bug too. And, as I said before, Waterfall began to dominate the way we thought.

It dominated, but it didn't work. For the next thirty years I, my associates, and my brother and sister programmers around the world, tried and tried and tried to get that analysis and design right. But every time we thought we had it, it slipped through our fingers during the implementation phase. All our months of careful planning were made irrelevant by the inevitable mad dash, made before the glaring eyes of managers and customers, to terribly delayed deadlines.

Despite the virtually unending stream of failures, we persisted in the Waterfall mindset. After all, how could this fail? How could thoroughly analyzing the problem, carefully designing a solution, and then implementing that design fail so spectacularly over and over again? It was inconceivable[6] that the problem lay in that strategy. The problem had to lie with us. Somehow, we were doing it wrong.

---

6. Watch *The Princess Bride* (1987) to hear the proper inflection of that word.

The level to which the Waterfall mindset dominated us can be seen in the language of the day. When Dijkstra came up with Structured Programming in 1968, Structured Analysis[7] and Structured Design[8] were not far behind. When Object-Oriented Programming (OOP) started to become popular in 1988, Object-Oriented Analysis[9] and Object-Oriented Design[10] (OOD) were also not far behind. This triplet of memes, this triumvirate of phases, had us in its thrall. We simply could not conceive of a different way to work.

And then, suddenly, we could.

The beginnings of the Agile reformation began in the late 1980s or early 1990s. The Smalltalk community began showing signs of it in the '80s. There were hints of it in Booch's 1991 book on OOD.[10] More resolution showed up in Cockburn's Crystal Methods in 1991. The Design Patterns community started to discuss it in 1994, spurred by a paper written by James Coplien.[11]

By 1995 Beedle,[12] Devos, Sharon, Schwaber, and Sutherland had written their famous paper on Scrum.[13] And the floodgates were opened. The bastion of Waterfall had been breached, and there was no turning back.

This, once again, is where I come into the story. What follows is from my memory, and I have not tried to verify it with the others involved. You should therefore assume that this recollection of mine has many omissions and

---

7. DeMarco, T. 1979. *Structured Analysis and System Specification*. Upper Saddle River, NJ: Yourdon Press.

8. Page-Jones, M. 1980. *The Practical Guide to Structured Systems Design*. Englewood Cliffs, NJ: Yourdon Press.

9. Coad, P., and E. Yourdon. 1990. *Object-Oriented Analysis*. Englewood Cliffs, NJ: Yourdon Press.

10. Booch, G. 1991. *Object Oriented Design with Applications*. Redwood City, CA: Benjamin-Cummings Publishing Co.

11. Coplien, J. O. 1995. A generative development-process pattern language. *Pattern Languages of Program Design*. Reading, MA: Addison-Wesley, p. 183.

12. Mike Beedle was murdered on March 23, 2018, in Chicago by a mentally disturbed homeless man who had been arrested and released 99 times before. He should have been institutionalized. Mike Beedle was a friend of mine.

13. Beedle, M., M. Devos, Y. Sharon, K. Schwaber, and J. Sutherland. SCRUM: An extension pattern language for hyperproductive software development. Accessed at http://jeffsutherland.org/scrum/scrum_plop.pdf.

contains much that is apocryphal, or at least wildly inaccurate. But Don't Panic, because I've at least tried to keep it a bit entertaining.

I first met Kent Beck at that 1994 PLOP,[14] where Coplien's paper was presented. It was a casual meeting, and nothing much came of it. I met him next in February 1999 at the OOP conference in Munich. But by then I knew a lot more about him.

At the time, I was a C++ and OOD consultant, flying hither and yon helping folks to design and implement applications in C++ using OOD techniques. My customers began to ask me about process. They had heard that Waterfall didn't mix with OO, and they wanted my advice. I agreed[15] about the mixing of OO and Waterfall and had been giving this idea a lot of thought myself. I had even thought I might write my own OO process. Fortunately, I abandoned that effort early on because I had stumbled across Kent Beck's writings on Extreme Programming (XP).

The more I read about XP, the more fascinated I was. The ideas were revolutionary (or so I thought at the time). They made sense, especially in an OO context (again, so I thought at the time). And so I was eager to learn more.

To my surprise, at that OOP conference in Munich, I found myself teaching across the hall from Kent Beck. I bumped into him during a break and said that we should meet for lunch to discuss XP. That lunch set the stage for a significant partnership. My discussions with him led me to fly out to his home in Medford, Oregon, to work with him to design a course about XP. During that visit, I got my first taste of Test-Driven Development (TDD) and was hooked.

At the time, I was running a company named Object Mentor. We partnered with Kent to offer a five-day boot camp course on XP that we called *XP Immersion*. From late 1999 until September 11, 2001,[16] they were a big hit! We trained hundreds of folks.

---

14. Pattern Languages of Programming was a conference held in the 1990s near the University of Illinois.
15. This is one of those strange coincidences that occur from time to time. There is nothing special about OO that makes it less likely to mix with Waterfall, and yet that meme was gaining a lot of traction in those days.
16. The significance of that date should not be overlooked.

In the summer of 2000, Kent invited a quorum of folks from the XP and Patterns community to a meeting near his home. He called it the "XP Leadership" meeting. We rode boats on, and hiked the banks of, the Rogue River. And we met to decide just what we wanted to do about XP.

One idea was to create a nonprofit organization around XP. I was in favor of this, but many were not. They had apparently had an unfavorable experience with a similar group founded around the Design Patterns ideas. I left that session frustrated, but Martin Fowler followed me out and suggested that we meet later in Chicago to talk it out. I agreed.

So Martin and I met in the fall of 2000 at a coffee shop near the ThoughtWorks office where he worked. I described to him my idea to get all the competing lightweight process advocates together to form a manifesto of unity. Martin made several recommendations for an invitation list, and we collaborated on writing the invitation. I sent the invitation letter later that day. The subject was *Light Weight Process Summit*.

One of the invitees was Alistair Cockburn. He called me to say that he was just about to call a similar meeting, but that he liked our invitation list better than his. He offered to merge his list with ours and do the legwork to set up the meeting if we agreed to have the meeting at Snowbird ski resort, near Salt Lake City.

Thus, the meeting at Snowbird was scheduled.

SNOWBIRD

I was quite surprised that so many people agreed to show up. I mean, who really wants to attend a meeting entitled, "The Light Weight Process Summit"? But here we all were, up in the Aspen room at the Lodge at Snowbird.

There were 17 of us. We have since been criticized for being 17 middle-aged white men. The criticism is fair up to a point. However, at least one woman,

Agneta Jacobson, had been invited but could not attend. And, after all, the vast majority of senior programmers in the world, at the time, were middle-aged white men—the reasons why this was the case is a story for a different time, and a different book.

The 17 of us represented quite a few different viewpoints, including 5 different lightweight processes. The largest cohort was the XP team: Kent Beck, myself, James Grenning, Ward Cunningham, and Ron Jeffries. Next came the Scrum team: Ken Schwaber, Mike Beedle, and Jeff Sutherland. Jon Kern represented Feature-Driven Development, and Arie van Bennekum represented the Dynamic Systems Development Method (DSDM). Finally, Alistair Cockburn represented his Crystal family of processes.

The rest of the folks were relatively unaffiliated. Andy Hunt and Dave Thomas were the Pragmatic Programmers. Brian Marick was a testing consultant. Jim Highsmith was a software management consultant. Steve Mellor was there to keep us honest because he was representing the Model-Driven philosophy, of which many of the rest of us were suspicious. And finally came Martin Fowler, who although he had close personal connections to the XP team, was skeptical of any kind of branded process and sympathetic to all.

I don't remember much about the two days that we met. Others who were there remember it differently than I do.[17] So, I'll just tell you what I remember, and I'll advise you to take it as the nearly two-decade-old recollection of a 65-year-old man. I might miss a few details, but the gist is probably correct.

It was agreed, somehow, that I would kick off the meeting. I thanked everyone for coming and suggested that our mission should be the creation of a manifesto that described what we believed to be in common about all these

---

17. There was a recently published history of the event in *The Atlantic:* Mimbs Nyce, C. 2017. The winter getaway that turned the software world upside down. *The Atlantic*. Dec 8. Accessed at https://www.theatlantic.com/technology/archive/2017/12/agile-manifesto-a-history/547715/. As of this writing I have not read that article, because I don't want it to pollute the recollection I am writing here.

lightweight processes and software development in general. Then I sat down. I believe that was my sole contribution to the meeting.

We did the standard sort of thing where we write issues down on cards and then sorted the cards on the floor into affinity groupings. I don't really know if that led anywhere. I just remember doing it.

I don't remember whether the magic happened on the first day or on the second. It seems to me it was toward the end of the first day. It may have been the affinity groupings that identified the four values, which were Individuals and Interactions, Working Software, Customer Collaboration, and Responding to Change. Someone wrote these on the whiteboard at the front of the room and then had the brilliant idea to say that these are preferred, but do not replace, the complementary values of processes, tools, documentation, contracts, and plans.

This is the central idea of the Agile Manifesto, and no one seems to remember clearly who first put it on the board. I seem to recall that it was Ward Cunningham. But Ward believes it was Martin Fowler.

Look at the picture on the agilemanifesto.org web page. Ward says that he took this picture to record that moment. It clearly shows Martin at the board with many of the rest of us gathered around.[18] This lends credence to Ward's notion that it was Martin who came up with the idea.

On the other hand, perhaps it's best that we never really know.

Once the magic happened, the whole group coalesced around it. There was some wordsmithing, and some tweaking and tuning. As I recall, it was Ward who wrote the preamble: "We are uncovering better ways of developing software by doing it and helping others do it." Others of us made tiny

---

18. From left to right, in a semi-circle around Martin, that picture shows Dave Thomas, Andy Hunt (or perhaps Jon Kern), me (you can tell by the blue jeans and the Leatherman on my belt), Jim Highsmith, someone, Ron Jeffries, and James Grenning. There is someone sitting behind Ron, and on the floor by his shoe appears to be one of the cards we used in the affinity grouping.

alterations and suggestions, but it was clear that we were done. There was this feeling of closure in the room. No disagreement. No argument. Not even any real discussion of alternatives. Those four lines were it.

- **Individuals and interactions** over processes and tools.
- **Working software** over comprehensive documentation.
- **Customer collaboration** over contract negotiation.
- **Responding to change** over following a plan.

Did I say we were done? It felt like it. But of course, there were lots of details to figure out. For one thing, what were we going to call this thing that we had identified?

The name "Agile" was not a slam dunk. There were many different contenders. I happened to like "Light Weight," but nobody else did. They thought it implied "inconsequential." Others liked the word "Adaptive." The word "Agile" was mentioned, and one person commented that it was currently a hot buzzword in the military. In the end, though nobody really loved the word "Agile," it was just the best of a bunch of bad alternatives.

As the second day drew to a close, Ward volunteered to put up the agilemanifesto.org website. I believe it was his idea to have people sign it.

AFTER SNOWBIRD

The following two weeks were not nearly so romantic or eventful as those two days in Snowbird. They were mostly dominated by the hard work of hammering out the principles document that Ward eventually added to the website.

The idea to write this document was something we all agreed was necessary in order to explain and direct the four values. After all, the four values are the kinds of statements that everyone can agree with without actually changing anything about the way they work. The principles make it clear that those four values have consequences beyond their "Mom and apple pie" connotation.

I don't have a lot of strong recollections about this period other than that we emailed the document containing the principles back and forth between each other and repeatedly wordsmithed it. It was a lot of hard work, but I think we all felt that it was worth the effort. With that done, we all went back to our normal jobs, activities, and lives. I presume most of us thought that the story would end there.

None of us expected the huge groundswell of support that followed. None of us anticipated just how consequential those two days had been. But lest I get a swelled head over having been a part of it, I continually remind myself that Alistair was on the verge of calling a similar meeting. And that makes me wonder how many others were also on the verge. So I content myself with the idea that the time was ripe, and that if the 17 of us hadn't met on that mountain in Utah, some other group would have met somewhere else and come to a similar conclusion.

Agile Overview

How do you manage a software project? There have been many approaches over the years—most of them pretty bad. Hope and prayer are popular among those managers who believe that there are gods who govern the fate of software projects. Those who don't have such faith often fall back on motivational techniques such as enforcing dates with whips, chains, boiling oil, and pictures of people climbing rocks and seagulls flying over the ocean.

These approaches almost universally lead to the characteristic symptoms of software mismanagement: Development teams who are always late despite working too much overtime. Teams who produce products of obviously poor quality that do not come close to meeting the needs of the customer.

THE IRON CROSS

The reason that these techniques fail so spectacularly is that the managers who use them do not understand the fundamental physics of software projects. This physics constrains all projects to obey an unassailable trade-off called the *Iron Cross* of project management. Good, fast, cheap, done: Pick any three you like. You can't have the fourth. You can have a project that is good, fast, and cheap, but it won't get done. You can have a project that is done, cheap, and fast, but it won't be any good.

The reality is that a good project manager understands that these four attributes have coefficients. A good manager drives a project to be good enough, fast enough, cheap enough, and done as much as necessary. A good manager manages the coefficients on these attributes rather than demanding that all those coefficients are 100%. It is this kind of management that Agile strives to enable.

At this point I want to be sure that you understand that Agile is a framework that *helps* developers and managers execute this kind of pragmatic project management. However, such management is not made automatic, and there is no guarantee that managers will make appropriate decisions. Indeed, it is entirely possible to work within the Agile framework and still completely mismanage the project and drive it to failure.

CHARTS ON THE WALL

So how does Agile aid this kind of management? *Agile provides data.* An Agile development team produces just the kinds of data that managers need in order to make good decisions.

Consider Figure 1.2. Imagine that it is up on the wall in the project room. Wouldn't this be great?

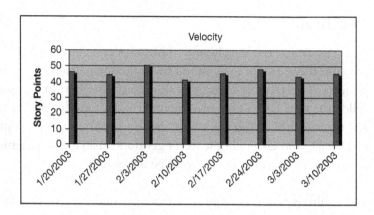

Figure 1.2 The team's velocity

This graph shows how much the development team has gotten done every week. The measurement unit is "points." We'll talk about what those points are later. But just look at that graph. Anyone can glance at that graph and see how fast the team is moving. It takes less than ten seconds to see that the average velocity is about 45 points per week.

Anyone, even a manager, can predict that next week the team will get about 45 points done. Over the next ten weeks, they ought to get about 450 points done. That's power! It's especially powerful if the managers and the team have a good feel for the number of points in the project. In fact, good Agile teams capture that information on yet another graph on the wall.

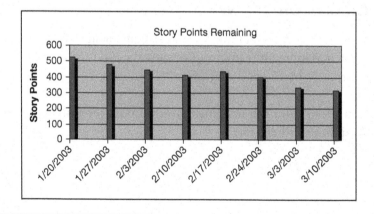

Figure 1.3 Burn-down chart

Figure 1.3 is called a *burn-down chart*. It shows how many points remain until the next major milestone. Notice how it declines each week. Note that it declines less than the number of points in the velocity chart. This is because there is a constant background of new requirements and issues being discovered during development.

Notice that the burn-down chart has a slope that predicts when the milestone will probably be reached. Virtually anyone can walk into the room, look at these two charts, and come to the conclusion that the milestone will be reached in June at a rate of 45 points per week.

Note that there is a glitch on the burn-down chart. The week of February 17 lost ground somehow. This might have been due to the addition of a new feature or some other major change to the requirements. Or it might have been the result of the developers re-estimating the remaining work. In either case, we want to know the effect on the schedule so that the project can be properly managed.

It is a critical goal of Agile to get those two charts on the wall. One of the driving motivations for Agile software development is to provide the data that managers need to decide how to set the coefficients on the Iron Cross and drive the project to the best possible outcome.

Many people would disagree with that last paragraph. After all, the charts aren't mentioned in the Agile Manifesto, nor do all Agile teams use such charts. And, to be fair, it's not actually the charts that matter. What matters is the data.

Agile development is first and foremost a feedback-driven approach. Each week, each day, each hour, and even each minute is driven by looking at the results of the previous week, day, hour, and minute, and then making the appropriate adjustments. This applies to individual programmers, and it also applies to the management of the entire team. Without data, the project cannot be managed.[19]

---

19. This is strongly related to John Boyd's OODA loop, summarized here: https://en.wikipedia.org/wiki/ OODA_loop. Boyd, J. R. 1987. *A Discourse on Winning and Losing.* Maxwell Air Force Base, AL: Air University Library, Document No. M-U 43947.

So even if you don't get those two charts on the wall, make sure you get the data in front of managers. Make sure the managers know how fast the team is moving and how much the team has left to accomplish. And present this information in a transparent, public, and obvious fashion—like putting the two charts on the wall.

But why is this data so important? Is it possible to effectively manage a project without that data? For 30 years we tried. And this is how it went...

THE FIRST THING YOU KNOW

What is the first thing you know about a project? Before you know the name of the project or any of the requirements, there is one piece of data that precedes all others. *The Date,* of course. And once *The Date* is chosen, *The Date* is frozen. There's no point trying to negotiate *The Date,* because *The Date* was chosen for good business reasons. If *The Date* is September, it's because there's a trade show in September, or there's a shareholders' meeting in September, or our funding runs out in September. Whatever the reason, it's a good *business* reason, and it's not going to change just because some developers think they might not be able to make it.

At the same time, the requirements are wildly in flux and can never be frozen. This is because the customers don't really know what they want. They sort of know what problem they want to *solve,* but translating that into the requirements of a system is never trivial. So the requirements are constantly being re-evaluated and re-thought. New features are added. Old features are removed. The UI changes form on a weekly if not daily basis.

This is the world of the software development team. It's a world in which dates are frozen and requirements are continuously changing. And somehow in that context, the development team must drive the project to a good outcome.

THE MEETING

The Waterfall model promised to give us a way to get our arms around this problem. To understand just how seductive and ineffective this was, I need to take you to *The Meeting.*

It is the first of May. The big boss calls us all into a conference room.

"We've got a new project," the big boss says. "It's got to be done November first. We don't have any requirements yet. We'll get them to you in the next couple of weeks."

"Now, how long will it take you to do the analysis?"

We look at each other out of the corner of our eyes. No one is willing to speak. How do you answer a question like that? One of us murmurs: "But we don't have any requirements yet."

"Pretend you have the requirements!" hollers the big boss. "You know how this works. You're all professionals. I don't need an exact date. I just need something to put in the schedule. Keep in mind if it takes any more than two months we might as well not do this project."

The words "Two months?" burble out of someone's mouth, but the big boss takes it as an affirmation. "Good! That's what I thought too. Now, how long will it take you to do the design?"

Again, astonished silence fills the room. You do the math. You realize that there are six months to November first. The conclusion is obvious. "Two months?" you say.

"Precisely!" the Big Boss beams. "Exactly what I thought. And that leaves us two months for the implementation. Thank you for coming to my meeting."

Many of you reading this have been to that meeting. Those of you who haven't, consider yourselves lucky.

THE ANALYSIS PHASE

So we all leave the conference room and return to our offices. What are we doing? This is the start of the Analysis Phase, so we must be analyzing. But just what is this thing called *analysis*?

If you read books on software analysis you'll find that there are as many definitions of analysis as there are authors. There is no real consensus on just what analysis is. It might be creating the work breakdown structure of the requirements. It might be the discovery and elaboration of the requirements. It might be the creation of the underlying data model, or object model, or... The best definition of analysis is: It's what analysts do.

Of course, some things are obvious. We should be sizing the project and doing basic feasibility and human resources projections. We should be ensuring that the schedule is achievable. That is the least that our business would be expecting of us. Whatever this thing called analysis is, it's what we are going to be doing for the next two months.

This is the honeymoon phase of the project. Everyone is happily surfing the web, doing a little day-trading, meeting with customers, meeting with users, drawing nice diagrams, and in general having a great time.

Then, on July 1, a miracle happens. We're done with analysis.

Why are we done with analysis? Because it's July 1. The schedule said we were supposed to be done on July 1, so we're done on July 1. Why be late?

So we have a little party, with balloons and speeches, to celebrate our passage through the phase gate and our entry into the Design Phase.

THE DESIGN PHASE

So now what are we doing? We are designing, of course. But just what is *designing*?

We have a bit more resolution about software design. Software design is where we split the project up into modules and design the interfaces between those modules. It's also where we consider how many teams we need and what the connections between those teams ought to be. In general, we are expected to refine the schedule in order to produce a realistically achievable implementation plan.

Of course, things change unexpectedly during this phase. New features are added. Old features are removed or changed. And we'd love to go back and re-analyze these changes; but time is short. So we just sort of hack these changes into the design.

And then another miracle happens. It's September 1, and we are done with the design. Why are we done with the design? Because it's September 1. The schedule says we are supposed to be done, so why be late?

So: another party. Balloons and speeches. And we blast through the phase gate into the Implementation Phase.

If only we could pull this off one more time. If only we could just *say* we were done with implementation. But we can't, because the thing about implementation is that is actually has to *be* done. Analysis and design are not *binary deliverables*. They do not have unambiguous completion criteria. There's no real way to know that you are done with them. So we might as well be done on time.

THE IMPLEMENTATION PHASE

Implementation, on the other hand, has definite completion criteria. There's no way to successfully pretend that it's done.[20]

It's completely unambiguous what we are doing during the Implementation Phase. We're coding. And we'd better be coding like mad banshees too, because we've already blown four months of this project.

Meanwhile, the requirements are still changing on us. New features are being added. Old features are being removed or changed. We'd love to go back and re-analyze and re-design these changes, but we've only got weeks left. And so we hack, hack, hack these changes into the code.

As we look at the code and compare it to the design, we realize that we must have been smoking some pretty special stuff when we did that design because the code sure isn't coming out anything like those nice pretty diagrams that

---

20. Though the developers of healthcare.gov certainly tried.

we drew. But we don't have time to worry about that because the clock is ticking and the overtime hours are mounting.

Then, sometime around October 15, someone says: "Hey, what's the date? When is this due?" That's the moment that we realize that there are only two weeks left and we're never going to get this done by November 1. This is also the first time that the stakeholders are told that there might be a small problem with this project.

You can imagine the stakeholders' angst. "Couldn't you have told us this in the Analysis Phase? Isn't that when you were supposed to be sizing the project and proving the feasibility of the schedule? Couldn't you have told us this during the Design Phase? Isn't that when you were supposed to be breaking up the design into modules, assigning those modules to teams, and doing the human resources projections? Why'd you have to tell us just two weeks before the deadline?"

And they have a point, don't they?

THE DEATH MARCH PHASE

So now we enter the Death March Phase of the project. Customers are angry. Stakeholders are angry. The pressure mounts. Overtime soars. People quit. It's hell.

Sometime in March, we deliver some limping thing that sort of half does what the customers want. Everybody is upset. Everybody is demotivated. And we promise ourselves that we will *never* do another project like this. Next time we'll do it right! Next time we'll do *more* analysis and *more* design.

I call this *Runaway Process Inflation*. We're going to do the thing that didn't work, and do a *lot* more of it.

HYPERBOLE?

Clearly that story was hyperbolic. It grouped together into one place nearly every bad thing that has ever happened in any software project. Most Waterfall projects did not fail so spectacularly. Indeed some, through sheer luck, managed to conclude with a modicum of success. On the other hand, I have been to that meeting on more than one occasion, and I have worked on more than one such project, and I am not alone. The story may have been hyperbolic, but it was still real.

If you were to ask me how many Waterfall projects were actually as disastrous as the one described above, I'd have to say relatively few—on the other hand, it's not zero, and it's far too many. Moreover, the vast majority suffered similar problems to a lesser (or sometimes greater) degree.

Waterfall was not an absolute disaster. It did not crush every software project into rubble. But it was, and remains, a disastrous way to run a software project.

A BETTER WAY

The thing about the Waterfall idea is that it just makes so much sense. First, we analyze the problem, then we design the solution, and then we implement the design.

Simple. Direct. Obvious. And wrong.

The Agile approach to a project is entirely different from what you just read, but it makes just as much sense. Indeed, as you read through this I think you'll see that it makes much more sense than the three phases of Waterfall.

An Agile project begins with analysis, but it's an analysis that never ends. In the diagram in Figure 1.4 we see the whole project. At the right is the end date, November 1. Remember, the first thing you know is the date. We subdivide that time into regular increments called *iterations* or *sprints*.[21]

---

21. *Sprint* is the term used in Scrum. I dislike the term because it implies running as fast as possible. A software project is a marathon, and you don't want to sprint in a marathon.

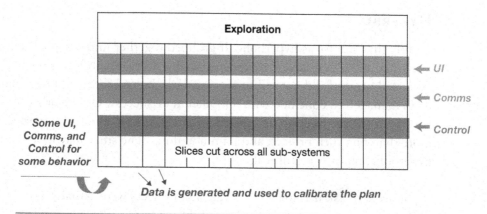

Figure 1.4 The whole project

The size of an iteration is typically one or two weeks. I prefer one week because too much can go wrong in two weeks. Other people prefer two weeks because they fear you can't get enough done in one week.

ITERATION ZERO

The first iteration, sometimes known as *Iteration Zero,* is used to generate a short list of features, called *stories.* We'll talk much more about this in future chapters. For now, just think of them as features that need to be developed. Iteration Zero is also used to set up the development environment, estimate the stories, and lay out the initial plan. That plan is simply a tentative allocation of stories to the first few iterations. Finally, Iteration Zero is used by the developers and architects to conjure up an initial tentative design for the system based on the tentative list of stories.

This process of writing stories, estimating them, planning them, and designing *never stops.* That's why there is a horizontal bar across the entire project named *Exploration.* Every iteration in the project, from the beginning to the end, will have some analysis and design and implementation in it. In an Agile project, we are *always* analyzing and designing.

Some folks take this to mean that Agile is just a series of mini-Waterfalls. That is *not* the case. Iterations are not subdivided into three sections. Analysis is not done solely at the start of the iteration, nor is the end of the iteration solely implementation. Rather, the activities of requirements analysis, architecture, design, and implementation are continuous throughout the iteration.

If you find this confusing, don't worry. Much more will be said about this in later chapters. Just keep in mind that iterations are not the smallest granule in an Agile project. There are many more levels. And analysis, design, and implementation occur in each of those levels. It's turtles all the way down.

AGILE PRODUCES DATA

Iteration one begins with an estimate of how many stories will be completed. The team then works for the duration of the iteration on completing those stories. We'll talk later about what happens inside the iteration. For now, what do you think the odds are that the team will finish all the stories that they planned to finish?

Pretty much zero, of course. That's because software is not a reliably estimable process. We programmers simply do not know how long things will take. This isn't because we are incompetent or lazy; it's because there is simply no way to know how complicated a task is going to be until that task is engaged and finished. But, as we'll see, all is not lost.

At the end of the iteration, some fraction of the stories that we had planned to finish will be done. This gives us our first measurement of how much can be completed in an iteration. This is *real data*. If we assume that every iteration will be similar, then we can use that data to adjust our original plan and calculate a new end date for the project (Figure 1.5).

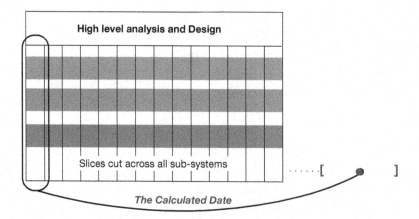

Figure I.5 Calculating the new end date

This calculation is likely to be very disappointing. It will almost certainly exceed the original end date for the project by a significant factor. On the other hand, this new date is based upon *real data,* so it should not be ignored. It also can't be taken too seriously yet because it is based on a single data point; the error bars around that projected date are pretty wide.

To narrow those error bars, we should do two or three more iterations. As we do, we get more data on how many stories can be done in an iteration. We'll find that this number varies from iteration to iteration but averages at a relatively stable *velocity.* After four or five iterations, we'll have a much better idea of when this project will be done (Figure 1.6).

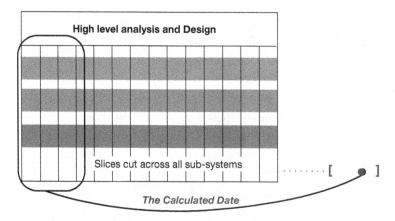

Figure I.6 More iterations mean a better idea of the project end date

As the iterations progress, the error bars shrink until there is no point in hoping that the original date has any chance of success.

HOPE VERSUS MANAGEMENT

This loss of hope is a major goal of Agile. We practice Agile in order to destroy hope before that hope can kill the project.

Hope is the project killer. Hope is what makes a software team mislead managers about their true progress. When a manager asks a team, "How's it going?" it is hope that answers: "Pretty good." Hope is a very bad way to manage a software project. And Agile is a way to provide an early and continuous dose of cold, hard reality as a replacement for hope.

Some folks think that Agile is about going fast. It's not. It's never been about going fast. Agile is about knowing, as early as possible, just how screwed we are. The reason we want to know this as early as possible is so that we can *manage* the situation. You see, *this* is what managers do. Managers *manage* software projects by gathering data and then making the best decisions they can based on that data. *Agile produces data.* Agile produces lots of data. Managers use that data to drive the project to the best possible outcome.

The best possible outcome is not often the originally desired outcome. The best possible outcome may be very disappointing to the stakeholders who originally commissioned the project. But the best possible outcome is, by definition, the best they are going to get.

MANAGING THE IRON CROSS

So now we return to the *Iron Cross* of project management: good, fast, cheap, done. Given the data produced by the project, it's time for the managers of that project to determine just how good, how fast, how cheap, and how done the project should be.

Managers do this by making changes to the scope, the schedule, the staff, and the quality.

Changing the Schedule

Let's start with the schedule. Let's ask the stakeholders if we can delay the project from November 1 to March 1. These conversations usually don't go well. Remember, the date was chosen for good business reasons. Those business reasons probably haven't changed. So a delay often means that the business is going to take a significant hit of some kind.

On the other hand, there are times when the business simply chooses the date for convenience. For example, maybe there is a trade show in November where they want to show off the project. Perhaps there's another trade show in March that would be just as good. Remember, it's still early. We're only a few iterations into this project. We want to tell the stakeholders that our delivery date will be March *before* they buy the booth space at the November show.

Many years ago, I managed a group of software developers working on a project for a telephone company. In the midst of the project, it became clear that we were going to miss the expected delivery date by six months. We confronted the telephone company executives about this as early as we could. These executives had never had a software team tell them, early, that the schedule would be delayed. They stood up and gave us a standing ovation.

You should not expect this. But it did happen to us. Once.

Adding Staff

In general, the business is simply not willing to change the schedule. The date was chosen for good business reasons, and those reasons still hold. So let's try to add staff. Everyone knows we can go twice as fast by doubling the staff.

Actually, this is exactly the opposite of the case. Brooks' law[22] states: *Adding manpower to a late project makes it later.*

---

22. Brooks, Jr., F. P. 1995 [1975]. *The Mythical Man-Month*. Reading, MA: Addison-Wesley. https://en.wikipedia.org/wiki/Brooks%27s_law.

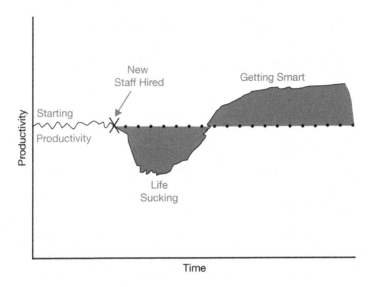

Figure 1.7 The actual effect of adding more members to the team

What really happens is more like the diagram in Figure 1.7. The team is working along at a certain productivity. Then new staff is added. Productivity plummets for a few weeks as the new people suck the life out of the old people. Then, hopefully, the new people start to get smart enough to actually contribute. The gamble that managers make is that the area under that curve will be net positive. Of course you need enough time, and enough improvement, to make up for the initial loss.

Another factor, of course, is that adding staff is expensive. Often the budget simply cannot tolerate hiring new people. So, for the sake of this discussion, let's assume that staff can't be increased. That means quality is the next thing to change.

Decreasing Quality

Everyone knows that you can go much faster by producing crap. So, stop writing all those tests, stop doing all those code reviews, stop all that refactoring nonsense, and just code you devils, just code. Code 80 hours per week if necessary, but just code!

I'm sure you know that I'm going to tell you this is futile. Producing crap does *not* make you go faster, it makes you go slower. This is *the* lesson you learn after you've been a programmer for 20 or 30 years. There is no such thing as quick and dirty. Anything dirty is slow.

> *The only way to go fast, is to go well.*

So we're going to take that quality knob and turn it up to 11. If we want to shorten our schedule, the only option is to *increase* quality.

Changing Scope

That leaves one last thing to change. Maybe, just maybe, some of the planned features don't really need to be done by November 1. Let's ask the stakeholders.

"Stakeholders, if you need all these features then it's going to be March. If you absolutely have to have something by November then you're going to have to take some features out."

"We're not taking anything out; we have to have it all! And we have to have it all by November first."

"Ah, but you don't understand. If you need it all, it's going to take us till March to do it."

"We need it all, and we need it all by November!"

This little argument will continue for a while because no one ever wants to give ground. But although the stakeholders have the moral high ground in this argument, the programmers have the data. And in any rational organization, the data will win.

If the organization is rational, then the stakeholders eventually bow their heads in acceptance and begin to scrutinize the plan. One by one, they will identify the features that they don't absolutely need by November. This hurts, but what real choice does the rational organization have? And so the plan is adjusted. Some features are delayed.

BUSINESS VALUE ORDER

Of course, inevitably the stakeholders will find a feature that we have already implemented and then say, "It's a real shame you did that one, we sure don't need it."

We never want to hear that again! So from now on, at the beginning of each iteration, we are going to ask the stakeholders which features to implement next. Yes, there are dependencies between the features, but we are *programmers,* we can deal with dependencies. One way or another we will implement the features in the order that the stakeholders ask.

HERE ENDETH THE OVERVIEW

What you have just read is the 20,000 foot view of Agile. A lot of details are missing, but this is the gist of it. Agile is a process wherein a project is subdivided into iterations. The output of each iteration is measured and used to continuously evaluate the schedule. Features are implemented in the order of business value so that the most valuable things are implemented first. Quality is kept as high as possible. The schedule is primarily managed by manipulating scope.

That's Agile.

CIRCLE OF LIFE

Figure 1.8 is Ron Jeffries' diagram describing the practices of XP. This diagram is affectionately known as the *Circle of Life.*

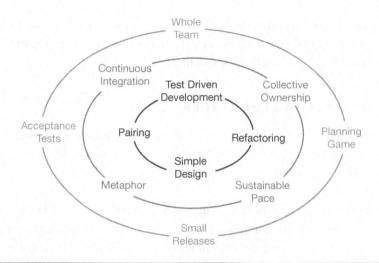

Figure 1.8 The Circle of Life

I have chosen the practices of XP for this book because, of all the Agile processes, XP is the best defined, the most complete, and the least muddled. Virtually all other Agile processes are a subset of or a variation on XP. This is not to say that these other Agile processes should be discounted. You may, in fact, find them valuable for various projects. But if you want to understand what Agile is really all about, there is no better way than to study XP. XP is the prototype, and the best representative, of the essential core of Agile.

Kent Beck is the father of XP, and Ward Cunningham is the grandfather. The two of them, working together at Tektronix in the mid '80s, explored many of the ideas that eventually became XP. Kent later refined those ideas into the concrete form that became XP, circa 1996. In 2000, Beck published the definitive work: *Extreme Programming Explained: Embrace Change.*[23]

The Circle of Life is subdivided into three rings. The outer ring shows the business-facing practices of XP. This ring is essentially the equivalent

---

23. Beck, K. 2000. *Extreme Programming Explained: Embrace Change*. Boston, MA: Addison-Wesley. There is a second edition with a 2005 copyright, but the first edition is my favorite and is the version that I consider to be definitive. Kent may disagree.

of the Scrum[24] process. These practices provide the framework for the way the software development team communicates with the business and the principles by which the business and development team manage the project.

- The *Planning Game* practice plays the central role of this ring. It tells us how to break down a project into features, stories, and tasks. It provides guidance for the estimation, prioritization, and scheduling of those features, stories, and tasks.
- *Small Releases* guides the team to work in bite-sized chunks.
- *Acceptance Tests* provide the definition of "done" for features, stories, and tasks. It shows the team how to lay down unambiguous completion criteria.
- *Whole Team* conveys the notion that a software development team is composed of many different functions, including programmers, testers, and managers, who all work together toward the same goal.

The middle ring of the Circle of Life presents the team-facing practices. These practices provide the framework and principles by which the development team communicates with, and manages, itself.

- *Sustainable Pace* is the practice that keeps a development team from burning their resources too quickly and running out of steam before the finish line.
- *Collective Ownership* ensures that the team does not divide the project into a set of knowledge silos.
- *Continuous Integration* keeps the team focused on closing the feedback loop frequently enough to know where they are at all times.
- *Metaphor* is the practice that creates and promulgates the vocabulary and language that the team and the business use to communicate about the system.

---

24. Or at least as Scrum was originally conceived. Nowadays, Scrum has absorbed many more of the XP practices.

The innermost ring of the Circle of Life represents the technical practices that guide and constrain the programmers to ensure the highest technical quality.

- *Pairing* is the practice that keeps the technical team sharing knowledge, reviewing, and collaborating at a level that drives innovation and accuracy.
- *Simple Design* is the practice that guides the team to prevent wasted effort.
- *Refactoring* encourages continual improvement and refinement of all work products.
- *Test Driven Development* is the safety line that the technical team uses to go quickly while maintaining the highest quality.

These practices align very closely with the goals of the Agile Manifesto in *at least* the following ways:

- **Individuals and interactions** over processes and tools
- Whole Team, Metaphor, Collective Ownership, Pairing, Sustainable Pace
- **Working software** over comprehensive documentation
- Acceptance Tests, Test Driven Development, Simple Design, Refactoring, Continuous Integration
- **Customer collaboration** over contract negotiation
- Small Releases, Planning Game, Acceptance Tests, Metaphor
- **Responding to change** over following a plan
- Small Releases, Planning Game, Sustainable Pace, Test Driven Development, Refactoring, Acceptance Tests

But, as we'll see as this book progresses, the linkages between the Circle of Life and the Agile Manifesto are much deeper and more subtle than the simple preceding model.

CONCLUSION

So that's what Agile is, and that's how Agile began. Agile is a small discipline that helps small software teams manage small projects. But despite all that smallness, the implications and repercussions of Agile are enormous because all big projects are, after all, made from many small projects.

With every day that passes, software is ever more insinuated into the daily lives of a vast and growing subset of our population. It is not too extreme to say that software rules the world. But if software rules the world, it is Agile that best enables the development of that software.

THE REASONS FOR AGILE

2

JAMES MADISON

KOHNKE

Before we dive into the details of Agile development, I want to explain what's at stake. Agile development is important, not just to software development, but to our industry, our society, and ultimately our civilization.

Developers and managers are often attracted to Agile development for transient reasons. They might try it because it just somehow feels right to them, or perhaps they fell for the promises of speed and quality. These reasons are intangible, indistinct, and easily thwarted. Many people have dropped Agile development simply because they didn't immediately experience the outcome they thought were promised.

These evanescent reasons are not why Agile development is important. Agile development is important for much deeper philosophical and ethical reasons. Those reasons have to do with professionalism and the reasonable expectations of our customers.

PROFESSIONALISM

What drew me to Agile in the first place was the high commitment to discipline over ceremony. To do Agile right, you had to work in pairs, write tests first, refactor, and commit to simple designs. You had to work in short cycles, producing executable output in each. You had to communicate with business on a regular and continuous basis.

Look back at the Circle of Life and view each one of those practices as a *promise,* a *commitment,* and you'll see where I am coming from. For me, Agile development is a commitment to up my game—to be a professional, and to promote professional behavior throughout the industry of software development.

We in this industry sorely need to increase our professionalism. We fail too often. We ship too much crap. We accept too many defects. We make terrible trade-offs. Too often, we behave like unruly teenagers with a new credit card. In simpler times, these behaviors were tolerable because the stakes were relatively low. In the '70s and '80s and even into the '90s, the cost of software failure, though high, was limited and containable.

SOFTWARE IS EVERYWHERE

Today things are different.

Look around you, right now. Just sit where you are and look around the room. How many computers are in the room with you?

Here, let me do that. Right now, I am at my summer cabin in the north woods of Wisconsin. How many computers are in this room with me?

- 4: I'm writing this on a MacBook Pro with 4 cores. I know, they say 8, but I don't count "virtual" cores. I also won't count all the little ancillary processors in the MacBook.
- 1: My Apple Magic Mouse 2. I'm sure it has more than one processor in it, but I'll just count it as 1.
- 1: My iPad running Duet as a second monitor. I know there are lots of other little processors in the iPad, but I'll only count it as one.
- 1: My car key (!).
- 3: My Apple AirPods. One for each earpiece, and one for the case. There are probably more in there but…
- 1: My iPhone. Yeah, yeah, the real number of processors in the iPhone is probably above a dozen, but I'll keep it at one.
- 1: Ultrasonic motion detector in sight. (There are many more in the house, but only one that I can see.)
- 1: Thermostat.
- 1: Security panel.
- 1: Flat-screen TV.
- 1: DVD player.
- 1: Roku Internet TV streaming device.
- 1: Apple AirPort Express.
- 1: Apple TV.
- 5: Remote controls.
- 1: Telephone. (Yes, an actual telephone.)
- 1: Fake fireplace. (You should see all the fancy modes it's got!)

- 2: Old computer-controlled telescope, a Meade LX 200 EMC. One processor in the drive and another in the handheld control unit.
- 1: Thumb drive in my pocket.
- 1: Apple pencil.

I count at least 30 computers on my person and in this room with me. The real number is probably double that since most of the devices have multiple processors in them. But let's just stick with 30 for the moment.

What did you count? I'll bet that for most of you it came close to my 30. Indeed, I'll wager that most of the 1.3 billion people living in Western society are constantly near more than a dozen computers. That's new. In the early '90s, that number would have averaged closer to zero.

What do every single one of those nearby computers have in common? They all need to be programmed. They all need software—software written by us. And what, do you think, is the quality of that software?

Let me put this in a different light. How many times per day does your grandmother interact with a software system? For those of you who still have living grandmothers that number will likely be in the thousands, because in today's society you can't do anything without interacting with a software system. You can't

- Talk on the phone.
- Buy or sell anything.
- Use the microwave oven, refrigerator, or even the toaster.
- Wash or dry your clothes.
- Wash the dishes.
- Listen to music.
- Drive a car.
- File an insurance claim.
- Increase the temperature in the room.
- Watch TV.

But it's worse than that. Nowadays, in our society, virtually nothing of significance can be done without interacting with a software system. No law can be passed, enacted, or enforced. No government policy can be debated. No plane can be flown. No car can be driven. No missile launched. No ship sailed. Roads can't be paved, food can't be harvested, steel mills can't mill steel, auto factories can't make cars, candy companies can't make candy, stocks can't be traded…

Nothing gets done in our society without software. Every waking moment is dominated by software. Many of us even monitor our sleep with software.

WE RULE THE WORLD

Our society has become utterly and wholly dependent on software. Software is the life's blood that makes our society run. Without it, the civilization we currently enjoy would be impossible.

And who writes all that software? You and I. We, programmers, rule the world.

Other people think they rule the world, but then they hand the rules they've made to us and *we* write the actual rules that run in the machines that monitor and control virtually every activity of modern life.

We, programmers, rule the world.

And we are doing a pretty poor job of it.

How much of that software, that runs absolutely everything, do you think is properly tested? How many programmers can say that they have a test suite that *proves,* with a high degree of certainty, that the software they have written works?

Do the hundred million lines of code that run inside your car work? Have you found any bugs in it? I have. What about the code that controls the brakes, and the accelerator, and the steering? Any bugs in that? Is there a test suite that can be run at a moment's notice that *proves* with a high degree of certainty that when you put your foot on the brake pedal, the car will actually stop?

How many people have been killed because the software in their cars failed to heed the pressure of the driver's foot on the brake pedal? We don't know for sure, but the answer is *many.* In one 2013 case Toyota paid millions in damages because the software contained "possible bit flips, task deaths that would disable the fail-safes, memory corruption, single-point failures, inadequate protections against stack overflow and buffer overflow, single-fault containment regions, [and] thousands of global variables" all within "spaghetti code."[1]

Our software is now killing people. You and I probably didn't get into this business to kill people. Many of us are programmers because, as kids, we wrote an infinite loop that printed our name on the screen, and we just thought that was so cool. But now our actions are putting lives and fortunes at stake. And with every passing day, more and more code puts more and more lives and fortunes at stake.

THE DISASTER

The day will come, if it hasn't already by the time you read this, when some poor programmer is going to do some dumb thing and kill ten thousand people in a single moment of carelessness. Think about that for a minute. It's not hard to imagine half a dozen scenarios. And when that happens, the politicians of the world will rise up in righteous indignation (as they should) and point their fingers squarely at us.

You might think that those fingers would point at our bosses, or the executives in our companies, but we saw what happened when those fingers pointed to the CEO of Volkswagen, North America, as he testified before Congress. The politicians asked him why Volkswagen had put software in their cars that purposely detected and defeated the emissions testing hardware

---

1. Safety Research & Strategies Inc. 2013. Toyota unintended acceleration and the big bowl of "spaghetti" code [blog post]. November 7. Accessed at http://www.safetyresearch.net/blog/articles/toyota-unintended-acceleration-and-big-bowl-%E2%80%9Cspaghetti%E2%80%9D-code.

used in California. He replied, "This was not a corporate decision, from my point of view, and to my best knowledge today. This was a couple of software engineers who put this in for whatever reasons."[2]

So, those fingers will point at us. And rightly so. Because it will have been our fingers on the keyboards, our disciplines that were lacking, and our carelessness that was the ultimate cause.

It was with this in mind that I held such high hopes for Agile. I hoped then, as I hope today, that the disciplines of Agile software development would be our first step toward turning computer programming into a true and honorable profession.

REASONABLE EXPECTATIONS

What follows is a list of perfectly reasonable expectations that managers, users, and customers have of us. Notice as you read through this list that one side of your brain agrees that each item is perfectly reasonable. Notice that the other side of your brain, the programmer side, reacts in horror. The programmer side of your brain may not be able to imagine how to meet these expectations.

Meeting these expectations is one of the primary goals of Agile development. The principles and practices of Agile address most of the expectations on this list quite directly. The behaviors below are what any good chief technology officer (CTO) should expect from their staff. Indeed, to drive this point home, I want you to think of me as your CTO. Here is what I expect.

WE WILL NOT SHIP SHYT!

It is an unfortunate aspect of our industry that this expectation even has to be mentioned. But it does. I'm sure, dear readers, that many of you have fallen afoul of this expectation on one or more occasions. I certainly have.

---

2. O'Kane, S. 2015. Volkswagen America's CEO blames software engineers for emissions cheating scandal. *The Verge.* October 8. Accessed at https://www.theverge.com/2015/10/8/9481651/volkswagen-congressional-hearing-diesel-scandal-fault.

To understand just how severe this problem is, consider the shutdown of the Air Traffic Control network over Los Angeles due to the rollover of a 32-bit clock. Or the shutdown of all the power generators on board the Boeing 787 for the same reason. Or the hundreds of people killed by the 737 Max MCAS software.

Or how about my own experience with the early days of healthcare.gov? After initial login, like so many systems nowadays, it asked for a set of security questions. One of those was "A memorable date." I entered 7/21/73, my wedding anniversary. The system responded with `Invalid Entry`.

I'm a programmer. I know how programmers think. So I tried many different date formats: `07/21/1973`, `07-21-1973`, `21 July, 1973`, `07211973`, etc. All gave me the same result. `Invalid Entry`. This was frustrating. What date format did the blasted thing want?

Then it occurred to me. The programmer who wrote this didn't know what questions would be asked. He or she was just pulling the questions from a database and storing the answers. That programmer was probably also disallowing special characters and numbers in those answers. So I typed: `Wedding Anniversary`. This was accepted.

I think it's fair to say that any system that requires its users to think like programmers in order to enter data in the expected format is crap.

I could fill this section with anecdotes about crappy software like this. But others have done this far better than I could. If you want to get a much better idea of the scope of this issue, read Gojko Adzic's book *Humans vs. Computers*[3] and Matt Parker's *Humble Pi*.[4]

It is perfectly reasonable for our managers, customers, and users to expect that we will provide systems for them that are high in quality and low in

---

3. Adzic, G. 2017. *Humans vs. Computers*. London: Neuri Consulting LLP. Accessed at http://humansvscomputers.com.

4. Parker, M. 2019. *Humble Pi: A Comedy of Maths Errors*. London: Penguin Random House UK. Accessed at https://mathsgear.co.uk/products/humble-pi-a-comedy-of-maths-errors.

defect. Nobody expects to be handed crap—especially when they pay good money for it.

Note that Agile's emphasis on Testing, Refactoring, Simple Design, and customer feedback is the obvious remedy for shipping bad code.

CONTINUOUS TECHNICAL READINESS

The last thing that customers and managers expect is that we, programmers, will create artificial delays to shipping the system. But such artificial delays are common in software teams. The cause of such delays is often the attempt to build all features simultaneously instead of the most important features first. So long as there are features that are half done, or half tested, or half documented, the system cannot be deployed.

Another source of artificial delays is the notion of stabilization. Teams will frequently set aside a period of continuous testing during which they watch the system to see if it fails. If no failures are detected after X days, the developers feel safe to recommend the system for deployment.

Agile resolves these issues with the simple rule that the system should be *technically* deployable at the end of every iteration. Technically deployable means that from the developers' points of view the system is technically solid enough to be deployed. The code is clean and the tests all pass.

This means that the work completed in the iteration includes all the coding, all the testing, all the documentation, and all the stabilization for the stories implemented in that iteration.

If the system is *technically* ready to deploy at the end of every iteration, then deployment is a *business decision,* not a technical decision. The business may decide there aren't enough features to deploy, or they may decide to delay deployment for market reasons or training reasons. In any case, the system quality meets the *technical* bar for deployability.

Is it possible for the system to be technically deployable every week or two? Of course it is. The team simply has to pick a batch of stories that is small enough to allow them to complete all the deployment readiness tasks before the end of the iteration. They'd better be automating the vast majority of their testing, too.

From the point of view of the business and the customers, continuous technical readiness is simply expected. When the business sees a feature work, they expect that feature is done. They don't expect to be told that they have to wait a month for QA stabilization. They don't expect that the feature only worked because the programmers driving the demo bypassed all the parts that don't work.

STABLE PRODUCTIVITY

You may have noticed that programming teams can often go very fast in the first few months of a greenfield project. When there's no existing code base to slow you down, you can get a lot of code working in a short time.

Unfortunately, as time passes, the messes in the code can accumulate. If that code is not kept clean and orderly, it will put a back pressure on the team that slows progress. The bigger the mess, the higher the back pressure, and the slower the team. The slower the team, the greater the schedule pressure, and the greater the incentive to make an even bigger mess. That positive-feedback loop can drive a team to near immobility.

Managers, puzzled by this slowdown, may finally decide to add human resources to the team in order to increase productivity. But as we saw in the previous chapter, adding personnel actually slows down the team for a few weeks.

The hope is that after those weeks the new people will come up to speed and help to increase the velocity. But who is training the new people? The people who made the mess in the first place. The new people will certainly emulate that established behavior.

Worse, the existing code is an even more powerful instructor. The new people will look at the old code and surmise how things are done in this team, and they will continue the practice of making messes. So the productivity continues to plummet despite the addition of the new folks.

Management might try this a few more times because repeating the same thing and expecting different results is the definition of management sanity in some organizations. In the end, however, the truth will be clear. Nothing that managers do will stop the inexorable plunge towards immobility.

In desperation, the managers ask the developers what can be done to increase productivity. And the developers have an answer. They have known for some time what needs to be done. They were just waiting to be asked.

"Redesign the system from scratch." The developers say.

Imagine the horror of the managers. Imagine the money and time that has been invested so far into this system. And now the developers are recommending that the whole thing be thrown away and redesigned from scratch!

Do those managers believe the developers when they promise, "This time things will be different"? Of course they don't. They'd have to be fools to believe that. Yet, what choice do they have? Productivity is on the floor. The business isn't sustainable at this rate. So, after much wailing and gnashing of teeth, they agree to the redesign.

A cheer goes up from the developers. "Hallelujah! We are all going back to the beginning when life is good and code is clean!" Of course, that's not what happens at all. What really happens is that the team is split in two. The ten best, The Tiger Team—the guys who made the mess in the first place—are chosen and moved into a new room. They will lead the rest of us into the golden land of a redesigned system. The rest of us hate those guys because now we're stuck maintaining the old crap.

From where does the Tiger Team get their requirements? Is there an up-to-date requirements document? Yes. It's the old code. The old code is the only document that accurately describes what the redesigned system should do.

So now the Tiger Team is poring over the old code trying to figure out just what it does and what the new design ought to be. Meanwhile the rest of us are changing that old code, fixing bugs and adding new features.

Thus, we are in a race. The Tiger Team is trying to hit a moving target. And, as Zeno showed in the parable of Achilles and the tortoise, trying to catch up to a moving target can be a challenge. Every time the Tiger Team gets to where the old system was, the old system has moved on to a new position.

It requires calculus to prove that Achilles will eventually pass the tortoise. In software, however, that math doesn't always work. I worked at a company where ten years later the new system had not yet been deployed. The customers had been promised a new system eight years before. But the new system never had enough features for those customers; the old system always did more than the new system. So the customers refused to take the new system.

After a few years, customers simply ignored the promise of the new system. From their point of view that system didn't exist, and it never would.

Meanwhile, the company was paying for two development teams: the Tiger Team and the maintenance team. Eventually, management got so frustrated that they told their customers they were deploying the new system despite their objections. The customers threw a fit over this, but it was nothing compared to the fit thrown by the developers on the Tiger Team—or, should I say, the remnants of the Tiger Team. The original developers had all been promoted and gone off to management positions. The current members of the team stood up in unison and said, "You can't ship this, it's crap. It needs to be redesigned."

OK, yes, another hyperbolic story told by Uncle Bob. The story is based on truth, but I did embellish it for effect. Still, the underlying message is entirely true. Big redesigns are horrifically expensive and seldom are deployed.

Customers and managers don't expect software teams to slow down with time. Rather, they expect that a feature similar to one that took two weeks at the start of a project will take two weeks a year later. They expect productivity to be stable over time.

Developers should expect no less. By continuously keeping the architecture, design, and code as clean as possible, they can keep their productivity high and prevent the otherwise inevitable spiral into low productivity and redesign.

As we will show, the Agile practices of Testing, Pairing, Refactoring, and Simple Design are the technical keys to breaking that spiral. And the Planning Game is the antidote to the schedule pressure that drives that spiral.

INEXPENSIVE ADAPTABILITY

Software is a compound word. The word "ware" means "product." The word "soft" means easy to change. Therefore, software is a product that is easy to change. Software was invented because we wanted a way to quickly and easily change the behavior of our machines. Had we wanted that behavior to be hard to change, we would have called it hardware.

Developers often complain about changing requirements. I have often heard statements like, "That change completely thwarts our architecture." I've got some news for you, sunshine. If a change to the requirements breaks your architecture, then your architecture sucks.

We developers should celebrate change because that's why we are here. Changing requirements is the name of the whole game. Those changes are the justification for our careers and our salaries. Our jobs depend on our ability to accept and engineer changing requirements and to make those changes relatively inexpensive.

To the extent that a team's software is hard to change, that team has thwarted the very reason for that software's existence. Customers, users, and managers expect that software systems will be easy to change and that the cost of such changes will be small and proportionate.

We will show how the Agile practices of TDD, Refactoring, and Simple Design all work together to make sure that software systems can be safely changed with a minimum of effort.

CONTINUOUS IMPROVEMENT

Humans make things better with time. Painters improve their paintings, songwriters improve their songs, and homeowners improve their homes. The same should be true for software. The older a software system is, the *better* it should be.

The design and architecture of a software system should get better with time. The structure of the code should improve, and so should the efficiency and throughput of the system. Isn't that obvious? Isn't that what you would expect from any group of humans working on anything?

It is the single greatest indictment of the software industry, the most obvious evidence of our failure as professionals, that we make things worse with time. The fact that we developers expect our systems to get messier, cruftier, and more brittle and fragile with time is, perhaps, the most irresponsible attitude possible.

Continuous, steady improvement is what users, customers, and managers expect. They expect that early problems will fade away and that the system will get better and better with time. The Agile practices of Pairing, TDD, Refactoring, and Simple Design strongly support this expectation.

FEARLESS COMPETENCE

Why don't most software systems improve with time? Fear. More specifically, fear of change.

Imagine you are looking at some old code on your screen. Your first thought is, "This is ugly code, I should clean it." Your next thought is, "I'm not touching it!" Because you know if you touch it, you will break it; and if you break it, it will become yours. So you back away from the one thing that might improve the code: cleaning it.

This is a fearful reaction. You fear the code, and this fear forces you to behave incompetently. You are incompetent to do the necessary cleaning because you fear the outcome. You have allowed this code, which you created, to go so far out of your control that you fear any action to improve it. This is irresponsible in the extreme.

Customers, users, and managers expect *fearless competence*. They expect that if you see something wrong or dirty, you will fix and clean it. They don't expect you to allow problems to fester and grow; they expect you to stay on top of the code, keeping it as clean and clear as possible.

So how do you eliminate that fear? Imagine that you own a button that controls two lights: one red, the other green. Imagine that when you push this button, the green light is lit if the system works, and the red light is lit if the system is broken. Imagine that pushing that button and getting the result takes just a few seconds. How often would you push that button? You'd never stop. You'd push that button all the time. Whenever you made any change to the code, you'd push that button to make sure you hadn't broken anything.

Now imagine that you are looking at some ugly code on your screen. Your first thought is, "I should clean it." And then you simply start to clean it, pushing the button after each small change to make sure you haven't broken anything.

The fear is gone. You can clean the code. You can use the Agile practices of Refactoring, Pairing, and Simple Design to improve the system.

How do you get that button? The Agile practice of TDD provides that button for you. If you follow that practice with discipline and determination, you will have that button, and you will be fearlessly competent.

QA SHOULD FIND NOTHING

QA should find no faults with the system. When QA runs their tests, they should come back saying that everything works as required. Any time QA finds a problem, the development team should find out what went wrong in their process and fix it so that next time QA will find nothing.

QA should wonder why they are stuck at the back end of the process checking systems that always work. And, as we shall see, there is a much better place for QA to be positioned.

The Agile practices of Acceptance Tests, TDD, and Continuous Integration support this expectation.

TEST AUTOMATION

The hands you see in the picture in Figure 2.1 are the hands of a QA manager. The document that manager is holding is *the table of contents* for a *manual test plan*. It lists 80,000 manual tests that must be run every six months by an army of testers in India. It costs over a million dollars to run those tests.

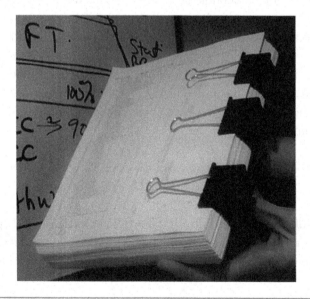

Figure 2.1   Table of contents for the manual test plan

The QA manager is holding this document out to me because he just got back from his boss' office. His boss just got back from the CFO's office. The year is 2008. The great recession has begun. The CFO cut that million dollars in half every six months. The QA manager is holding this document out to me asking me which half of these tests he shouldn't run.

I told him that no matter how he decided to cut the tests, he wouldn't know if half of his system was working.

This is the inevitable result of manual testing. Manual tests are always eventually lost. What you just heard was the first and most obvious mechanism for losing manual tests: manual tests are *expensive* and so are always a target for reduction.

However, there is a more insidious mechanism for losing manual tests. Developers seldom deliver to QA on time. This means that QA has less time than planned to run the tests they need to run. So, QA must *choose* which tests they believe are most appropriate to run in order to make the shipment deadline. And so some tests aren't run. They are lost.

And besides, humans are not machines. Asking humans to do what machines can do is expensive, inefficient, and *immoral*. There is a much better activity for which QA should be employed—an activity that uses their human creativity and imagination. But we'll get to that.

Customers and users expect that every new release is thoroughly tested. No one expects the development team to bypass tests just because they ran out of time or money. So every test that can feasibly be automated must be automated. Manual testing should be limited to those things that cannot be automatically validated and to the creative discipline of Exploratory Testing.[5]

The Agile practices of TDD, Continuous Integration, and Acceptance Testing support this expectation.

---

5. Agile Alliance. Exploratory testing. Accessed at https://www.agilealliance.org/glossary/exploratory-testing.

WE COVER FOR EACH OTHER

As CTO, I expect development teams to behave like teams. How do teams behave? Imagine a team of players moving the ball down the field. One of the players trips and falls. What do the other players do? They cover the open hole left behind by the fallen team member *and continue to move the ball down the field*.

On board a ship, everyone has a job. Everyone also knows how to do someone else's job. Because on board the ship, all jobs must get done.

In a software team, if Bob gets sick, Jill steps in to finish Bob's tasks. This means that Jill had better know what Bob was working on and where Bob keeps all the source files, and scripts, etc.

I expect that the members of each software team will cover for each other. I expect that each individual member of a software team makes sure that there is someone who can cover for him if he goes down. It is *your* responsibility to make sure that one or more of your teammates can cover for you.

If Bob is the database guy, and Bob gets sick, I don't expect progress on the project to grind to a halt. Someone else, even though she isn't "the database guy," should pick up the slack. I don't expect the team to keep knowledge in silos; I expect knowledge to be shared. If I need to reassign half the members of the team to a new project, I do not expect that half the knowledge will be removed from the team.

The Agile practices of Pair Programming, Whole Team, and Collective Ownership support these expectations.

HONEST ESTIMATES

I expect estimates, and I expect them to be honest. The most honest estimate is "I don't know." However, that estimate is not complete. You may not know everything, but there are some things you do know. So I expect you to provide estimates based on what you do *and don't* know.

For example, you may not know how long something will take, but you can compare one task to another in relative terms. You may not know how long it will take to build the *Login* page, but you might be able to tell me that the *Change Password* page will take about half the time as *Login*. Relative estimates like that are immensely valuable, as we will see in a later chapter.

Or, instead of estimating in relative terms, you may be able to give me a range of probabilities. For example, you might tell me that the *Login* page will take anywhere from 5 to 15 days to complete with an average completion time of 12 days. Such estimates combine what you do *and don't* know into an honest probability for managers to manage.

The Agile practices of the Planning Game and Whole Team support this expectation.

You Need to Say "No"

While it is important to strive to find solutions to problems, I expect you to say "no" when no such solution can be found. You need to realize that you were hired more for your ability to say "no" than for your ability to code. You, programmers, are the ones who know whether something is possible. As your CTO, I am counting on you to inform us when we are headed off a cliff. I expect that, no matter how much schedule pressure you feel, no matter how many managers are demanding results, you will say "no" when the answer really is "no."

The Agile practice of Whole Team supports this expectation.

Continuous Aggressive Learning

As CTO, I expect you to keep learning. Our industry changes quickly. We must be able to change with it. So learn, learn, learn! Sometimes the company can afford to send you to courses and conferences. Sometimes the company can afford to buy books and training videos. But if not, then you must find ways to continue learning without the company's help.

The Agile practice of Whole Team supports this expectation.

MENTORING

As CTO I expect you to teach. Indeed, the best way to learn is to teach. So when new people join the team, teach them. Learn to teach each other.

Again, the Agile practice of Whole Team supports this expectation.

THE BILL OF RIGHTS

During the Snowbird meeting, Kent Beck said that the goal of Agile was to heal the divide between business and development. To that end, the following bill of rights was developed by Kent, Ward Cunningham, and Ron Jeffries, among others.

Notice, as you read these rights, that the rights of the customer and the rights of the developer are complementary. They fit together like a hand in a glove. They create a balance of expectations between the two groups.

CUSTOMER BILL OF RIGHTS

The customer bill of rights includes the following:

- You have the right to an overall plan and to know what can be accomplished when and at what cost.
- You have the right to get the most possible value out of every iteration.
- You have the right to see progress in a running system, proven to work by passing repeatable tests that you specify.
- You have the right to change your mind, to substitute functionality, and to change priorities without paying exorbitant costs.
- You have the right to be informed of schedule and estimate changes, in time to choose how to reduce the scope to meet a required date. You can cancel at any time and be left with a useful working system reflecting investment to date.

DEVELOPER BILL OF RIGHTS

The developer bill of rights includes the following:

- You have the right to know what is needed with clear declarations of priority.
- You have the right to produce high-quality work at all times.
- You have the right to ask for and receive help from peers, managers, and customers.
- You have the right to make and update your own estimates.
- You have the right to accept your responsibilities instead of having them assigned to you.

These are extremely powerful statements. We should consider each in turn.

CUSTOMERS

The word "customer" in this context refers to businesspeople in general. This includes true customers, managers, executives, project leaders, and anyone else who might carry responsibility for schedule and budget or who will pay for and benefit from the execution of the system.

> *Customers have the right to an overall plan and to know what can be accomplished when and at what cost.*

Many people have claimed that up-front planning is not part of Agile development. The very first customer right belies that claim. Of course the business needs a plan. Of course that plan must include schedule and cost. And, of course that plan should be as accurate and precise as practical.

It is in that last clause that we often get into trouble because the only way to be both accurate and precise is to actually develop the project. Being both accurate and precise by doing anything less is impossible. So what we developers must do to guarantee this right is to make sure that our plans, estimates, and schedules properly describe the level of our uncertainty and define the means by which that uncertainty can be mitigated.

In short, we cannot agree to deliver fixed scopes on hard dates. Either the scopes or the dates must be soft. We represent that softness with probability curve. For example, we estimate that there is a 95% probability that we can get the first ten stories done by the date. A 50% chance that we can get the next five done by the date. And a 5% chance that the five after that might get done by the date.

Customers have the right to this kind of probability-based plan because they cannot manage their business without it.

Customers have the right to get the most possible value out of every iteration.

Agile breaks up the development effort into fixed time boxes called *iterations*. The business has the right to expect that the developers will work on the most important things at any given time, and that each iteration will provide them the maximum possible *usable* business value. This priority of value is specified by the customer during the planning sessions at the beginning of each iteration. The customers choose the stories that give them the highest return on investment and that can fit within the developer's estimation for the iteration.

Customers have the right to see progress in a running system, proven to work by passing repeatable tests that they specify.

This seems obvious when you think about it from the customer's point of view. Of course they have the right to see incremental progress. Of course they have the right to specify the criteria for accepting that progress. Of course they have the right to quickly and repeatedly see proof that their acceptance criteria have been met.

Customers have the right to change their minds, to substitute functionality, and to change priorities without paying exorbitant costs.

After all, this is *soft*ware. The whole point of software is to be able to easily change the behavior of our machines. The softness is the reason software was invented in the first place. So of course, customers have the right to change the requirements.

Customers have the right to be informed of schedule and estimate changes in time to choose how to alter the scope to meet the required date.

Customers may cancel at any time and be left with a useful working system reflecting investment to date.

Note that customers do not have the right to demand conformance to the schedule. Their right is limited to managing the schedule by changing the scope. The most important thing this right confers is the right to *know* that the schedule is in jeopardy so that it can be managed in a timely fashion.

DEVELOPERS

In this context, developers are anyone who works on the development of code. This includes programmers, QA, testers, and business analysts.

Developers have the right to know what is needed with clear declarations of priority.

Again, the focus is on *knowledge*. Developers are entitled to precision in the requirements and in the importance of those requirements. Of course, the same constraint of *practicality* holds for requirements as holds for estimates. It is not always possible to be perfectly precise about requirements. And indeed, customers have the right to change their minds.

So this right only applies *within the context of an iteration*. Outside of an iteration, requirements and priorities will shift and change. But within an iteration the developers have the right to consider them immutable. Always remember, however, that developers may choose to waive that right if they consider a requested change to be inconsequential.

Developers have the right to produce high-quality work at all times.

This may be the most profound of all these rights. Developers have the right to do good work. The business has no right to tell developers to cut corners or do low-quality work. Or, to say this differently, the business has no right to force developers to ruin their professional reputations or violate their professional ethics.

Developers have the right to ask for and receive help from peers, managers, and customers.

This help comes in many forms. Programmers may ask each other for help solving a problem, checking a result, or learning a framework, among other things. Developers might ask customers to better explain requirements or to refine priorities. Mostly, this statement gives programmers the right to *communicate*. And with that right to ask for help comes the responsibility to give help when asked.

Developers have the right to make and update their own estimates.

No one can estimate a task for you. And if you estimate a task, you can always change your estimate when new factors come to light. Estimates are guesses. They are intelligent guesses to be sure, but they're still guesses. They are guesses that get better with time. Estimates are never commitments.

Developers have the right to accept their responsibilities instead of having them assigned.

Professionals *accept* work, they are not assigned work. A professional developer has every right to say "no" to a particular job or task. It may be that the developer does not feel confident in their ability to complete the task, or it may be that the developer believes the task better suited for someone else. Or, it may be that the developer rejects the tasks for personal or moral reasons.[6]

---

6. Consider the developers at Volkswagen who "accepted" the tasks of cheating the EPA test rigs in California. https://en.wikipedia.org/wiki/Volkswagen_emissions_scandal.

In any case, the right to accept comes with a cost. Acceptance implies responsibility. The accepting developer becomes responsible for the quality and execution of the task, for continually updating the estimate so that the schedule can be managed, for communicating status to the whole team, and for asking for help when help is needed.

Programming on a team involves working closely together with juniors and seniors. The team has the right to collaboratively decide who will do what. A technical leader might ask a developer to take a task but has no right to force a task on anyone.

CONCLUSION

Agile is a framework of disciplines that support professional software development. Those who profess these disciplines accept and conform to the reasonable expectations of managers, stakeholders, and customers. They also enjoy and abide by the rights that Agile confers to developers and customers. This mutual acceptance and conference of rights and expectations—this profession of disciplines—is the foundation of an *ethical* standard for software.

Agile is not a process. Agile is not a fad. Agile is not merely a set of rules. Rather, Agile is a set of rights, expectations, and disciplines of the kind that form the basis of an ethical profession.

BUSINESS 3 PRACTICES

There are a host of business-facing practices that development must follow in order to succeed. These include Planning, Small Releases, Acceptance Tests, and Whole Team.

PLANNING

How do you estimate a project? The simple answer is that you break it down into its constituent pieces and then estimate those pieces. This is a fine approach; but what if the pieces themselves are too big to estimate with any accuracy? You simply break down those pieces into smaller pieces and estimate them. I'm sure you can all smell the recursive descent.

How far down can you carry this procedure? You can carry it right down to individual lines of code. In fact, this is what programmers do. A programmer is someone who is skilled at breaking down a task into individual lines of code.

If you would like an accurate and precise estimate of a project, then break it down into individual lines of code. The time it takes you to do this will give you a *very* accurate and precise measure of how long it took you to build the project—because you just built it.

Of course, that misses the point of an *estimate*. An estimate is a guess; we want some idea of how long the project will take without actually *building* the project. We want the cost of estimation to be low. Therefore an estimate is, by definition, *imprecise*. The imprecision allows us to shorten the time necessary to create the estimate. The more imprecision, the less time the estimate will take.

This is not to say that an estimate should be *inaccurate*. Estimates should be as accurate as possible, but only as precise as necessary to keep the cost of estimation low. An example may help. I estimate the moment of my death to be sometime within the next thousand years. This is completely accurate, but very imprecise. It took me virtually no time at all to create this accurate estimate because the imprecision was so large. The imprecision of an accurate estimate denotes a range of time within which the estimated event will almost certainly occur.

The trick, for software developers, is to spend a small amount of time choosing the smallest range that remains accurate.

TRIVARIATE ANALYSIS

One technique that works quite well for large tasks is *trivariate estimation.* Such estimates are composed of three numbers: *best-case, nominal-case,* and *worst-case.* These numbers are *confidence* estimates. The *worst-case* number is the amount of time within which you feel 95% confident that the task will be completed. The *nominal-case* has only 50% confidence, and the *best-case* only 5%.

For example, I am 95% sure that the task will be completed within three weeks. I am only 50% sure that it will be completed in two weeks. And I am only 5% sure that it will be completed within one week.

Another way to think about this is that, given 100 similar tasks, five of them will be done within one week, 50 will be done within two weeks, and 95 of them will be done within three weeks.

There is a whole mathematical method surrounding the management of trivariate estimates. If you are interested, I encourage you to research the program evaluation and review technique (PERT).[1] It is a powerful method for managing large projects and portfolios of projects. And if you haven't studied this technique, don't assume that you know it already. There's a lot more to PERT than those Microsoft Project diagrams with which you may be familiar.

As powerful as trivariate analysis is for long-term estimation of a whole project, this technique is too imprecise for the day-to-day management that we need *within* a project. For that, we use another approach: *story points.*

---

1. https://en.wikipedia.org/wiki/Program_evaluation_and_review_technique

STORIES AND POINTS

The story point technique deals with accuracy and precision by using a very tight feedback loop that iteratively calibrates and recalibrates estimates against reality. Imprecision is high at first, but within a few cycles it is reduced to manageable levels. But before we get into that, we need to talk a bit about stories.

A *user story* is an abbreviated description of a feature of the system, told from the point of view of a user. So, for example:

> *As the driver of a car, in order to increase my velocity, I will press my foot harder on the accelerator pedal.*

This is one of the more common forms of a user story. Some people like it. Others prefer the more abbreviated form: *Accelerate.* Both work pretty well. Both are simply placeholders for a much larger conversation.

Much of that conversation has not happened yet. It will happen when the developers are on the verge of developing the feature. The conversation was begun, however, at the moment that the story was written. At that time, the developers and stakeholders talked over some of the possible details of the story and then chose a simple wording to write down.

The wording is simple, and the details are omitted because it is too early to count on those details. We want to delay the specification of those details as long as possible, right up to the point where the story is developed. So we leave the story in abbreviated form as a promise for a future conversation.[2]

Typically, we write the story on an index card. I know, I know. Why in the world would we use such ancient and primitive tools when we have computers and iPads and...? It turns out that being able to hold those cards in your hands, pass them across a table to each other, scribble on them, and otherwise *handle* them is immensely valuable.

---

2. This is one of Ron Jeffries' definitions of a story.

Automated tools do sometimes have their place, and I'll talk about them in another chapter. For the moment, however, think of the stories as index cards.

Please remember: World War II was managed[3] on index cards, so I think the technique scales.

ATM Stories

Imagine that it is Iteration Zero, and we are on a team writing the stories for an automated teller machine (ATM). What are these stories? The first few are pretty easy to figure out: *Withdrawal, Deposit,* and *Transfer.* Of course, you also have to identify yourself to the ATM. We might call that *Login.* And that implies that there is a way to *Logout.*

Now we have five cards. There will almost certainly be more once we start really getting into the behavior of the machine. We could imagine auditing tasks, loan payment tasks, and all kinds of other things. But let's stick with those first five for now.

What's on those cards? Just the words mentioned: *Login, Logout, Withdrawal, Deposit,* and *Transfer.* Of course, those aren't the only words that were *spoken* during our exploration. We talked about many details during that meeting. We mentioned how the user logs in by inserting her card in a slot and entering a PIN. We discussed a deposit consisting of an envelope that is inserted into a slot and on which we print identifying marks. We talked about how cash is dispensed, and what to do if the cash jams or if we run out. We worked through many of those details.

But we don't trust those details yet, so we don't write them down. What we write down are just the words. There's nothing wrong with making a few notes on the card if you want some reminders of the issues, but these aren't requirements. There's nothing formal on the cards.

---

3. Well, to some extent anyway.

This rejection of detail is a *discipline*. And it's hard. Everyone on the team will feel the need to capture all the details discussed in one way or another. Resist this urge!

I once worked with a project manager who absolutely insisted on writing down every detail about each and every story on the story card. The story cards were filled with paragraphs and paragraphs in tiny little print. They became impenetrable and unusable. They had so much detail on them they could not be estimated. They could not be scheduled. They were useless. Worse, there was so much effort invested into each story card that they could not be discarded.

What makes a story manageable, schedulable, and estimable is the temporary lack of detail. Stories must start out cheap because a lot of them are going to be modified, split, merged, or even discarded. Just keep reminding yourself that they are placeholders, not requirements.

Now we have a batch of story cards created in Iteration Zero. Others will be created later as new features and new ideas are encountered. In fact, the process of story creation never ends. Stories are always being written, changed, discarded, and (most importantly) developed over the course of the project.

Estimating the Stories

Imagine that these cards are on the table in front of you, and sitting around the table are other developers, testers, and stakeholders. You have all met in order to *estimate* these cards. There will be many meetings like this. They will be convened any time new stories are added or something new has been learned about old stories. Expect such meetings to be an informal but regular event in each iteration.

However, it's still early in Iteration Zero, and this estimation meeting is the first. None of the stories has yet been estimated.

So, we pick a story from the batch that we consider to be of average complexity. Perhaps it is the *Login* story. Many of us were there when the story was written, so we heard the kinds of details that the stakeholders imagined would be part of this story. We will likely ask the stakeholders to review those details now, just so that we all have the proper context.

Then, we choose a number of points for the story. The *Login* story will cost 3 points of development effort (Figure 3.1). Why 3? Why not? *Login* is an average story, and so we give it an average cost. Three is average if our stories range in cost from 1 to 6.

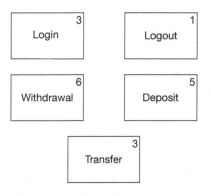

Figure 3.1 The Login story gets assigned three points

Login is now our *Golden Story*. It is the standard against which all other stories will be compared. So, for example, logging out is a lot simpler than logging in. We'll give the *Logout* story 1 point. *Withdrawal* is perhaps twice as hard as *Login,* so we'll say it's a 6. *Deposit* is similar to *Withdrawal* but perhaps not quite as hard, so we'll give it a 5. Finally, *Transfer* is about the same as *Login,* so we'll give it a 3.

We write these numbers up in one corner of each story card that we estimate. I'll talk much more about the estimation process later. For now, let's just say that we now have a batch of story cards with estimates on them that range from 1 to 6. Why 1 to 6? Why not? There are many schemes for assigning cost. The simpler ones are usually better.

At this point, you may be wondering what these points are really measuring. Perhaps you think they are hours, days, weeks, or some other unit of time.

They are not. Rather, they are a unit of estimated effort, not real time. They are not even estimated time—they are estimated *effort*.

Story points should be roughly linear. A card with a 2 should require about half the effort of a card with a 4. However, the linearity doesn't have to be perfect. Remember, these are *estimates,* so precision is kept intentionally wide. A story with a 3 might take Jim two days to implement if he doesn't get distracted by a bug in the field. Or it might take Pat only one day if she works at home on it. These numbers are vague, fuzzy, imprecise things that *do not relate* directly to real time.

But there is a beautiful thing about vague and fuzzy numbers. It's called the Law of Large Numbers.[4] When taken in quantity, the fuzziness integrates out! We're going to take advantage of that later.

Planning Iteration One

Meanwhile, it's time to plan the first iteration. The iteration begins with the *Iteration Planning Meeting* (IPM). This meeting should be scheduled to be one-twentieth the duration of the iteration. The IPM for a two-week iteration should require about a half a day.

The whole team attends the IPM. This includes the stakeholders, the programmers, the testers, and the project manager. The stakeholders will have previously read the estimated stories and sorted them in the order of business value. Some teams actually choose numbers for that business value, similar to the technique used for the story points. Other teams just eyeball the business value.

The job of the stakeholders at the IPM is to choose the stories that will be implemented by the programmers and testers during the iteration. To do this, they need to know how many story points the programmers think they can complete. This number is called the *velocity.* Of course, since this is the first iteration, no one has any real idea what the velocity is going to be. So the team makes a guess. Let's say that guess is 30.

---

4. https://en.wikipedia.org/wiki/Law_of_large_numbers

It's important to realize that velocity is not a commitment. The team is not making a promise to get 30 points done during the iteration. They aren't even making the promise to *try* to get 30 points done. This is nothing more than their best guess as to how many points will be complete by the end of the iteration. That guess is probably not very accurate.

Return on Investment

Now the stakeholders play the four-quadrant game (Figure 3.2).

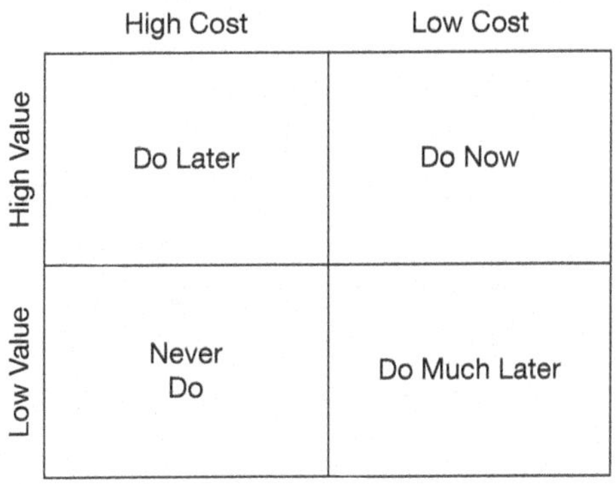

Figure 3.2 The four-quadrant game

The stories that are valuable but cheap will be done right away. Those that are valuable but expensive will be done later. Those that are neither valuable nor expensive might get done one day. Those that are not valuable but are expensive will never be done.

This is a *return on investment* (ROI) calculation. It's not made formally, and no math is necessary. The stakeholders simply look at the card and make a judgement based on its value and its estimated cost.

So, for example: "*Login* is pretty important; but it's also pretty expensive. Let's wait. *Logout* is important too, and it's quite cheap. Do it! *Withdrawal* is expensive—really expensive. But it's also important to show that feature off first. So do it."

That's how the process works. The stakeholders scan the deck of stories for those that have the highest bang for buck, the highest ROI. When they find enough to add up to 30 points, they stop. That's the plan for the iteration.

The Midpoint Check

Let's get to work. I'll explain the process involved in developing the stories in detail later. For now, just imagine that there is some procedure for turning stories into working code. Think of it as moving story cards from the *planned pile* to the *done pile*.

At the midpoint of the iteration, many stories should be done. What should the point total of those stories add up to? That's right, 15. To do this process, you must be able to divide by two.

So, let's call the midpoint review meeting. It's Monday morning, the first day of the second week of the iteration. The team gathers with the stakeholders, and they look at the progress.

Uh oh, the completed stories only add up to 10 points. With only a week left, it's not likely that they are going to get 20 more points done. So the stakeholders remove enough stories from the plan to reduce the remaining points to 10.

By Friday afternoon, the iteration concludes with a demo. It turns out only 18 points were completed. Has this iteration failed?

No! *Iterations do not fail*. The purpose of an iteration is to generate data for managers. It would be nice if the iteration also generated working code, but even when it doesn't it has still generated data.

Yesterday's Weather

Now we know how many points we can do in a week: about 18. On Monday, when the next iteration begins, how many points should the stakeholders plan for? Eighteen, of course. This is called *yesterday's weather*. The best predictor of today's weather is yesterday's weather. The best predictor of the progress of an iteration is the previous iteration.

So at the IPM, the stakeholders select stories that add up to 18 points. But this time, at the midpoint review, something strange has happened. There are 12 points done. Should we tell them?

We don't have to. They can see it for themselves. So the stakeholders add six more points to the plan, for a planned total of 24.

Of course, the team really only completes 22. So 22 will be chosen for the next iteration.

The End of the Project

And on it goes like this. As each iteration completes. the completed velocity is added to the velocity chart, so that everyone can see how fast the team is going.

Now imagine that this process continues, iteration after iteration, month after month. What is happening to that deck of story cards? Think of the iteration cycle as a pump that pumps the ROI out of that deck. Think of the continuous exploration of the requirements as a pump that pumps ROI back into the deck. As long as incoming ROI outpaces the outgoing ROI, the project will continue.

However, it may happen that the number of new features discovered in exploration gradually sinks to zero. When that happens, the remaining ROI in the deck will be exhausted after just a few more iterations. The day will come when, at the IPM, the stakeholders scan the deck for something worth doing and find nothing. The project is over.

The project is not over when all the stories are implemented. The project is over when there are no more stories in the deck worth implementing.

It is sometimes amazing what is left in the deck after the project is over. I once worked on a year-long project where the very first story written, the story that gave the project its name, was never chosen for implementation. That story was important at the time, but there were many more urgent stories to implement. By the time all those urgent stories were resolved, the importance of the original story had evaporated.

STORIES

User stories are simple statements that we use as reminders of features. We try not to record too much detail when we write the story because we know that those details will likely change. The details *are* recorded later, but as acceptance tests, which we'll discuss later.

Stories follow a simple set of guidelines that we remember with the acronym *INVEST*.

- **I: Independent.** User stories are independent of each other. This means that they do not need to be implemented in any particular order. *Login* does not need to be implemented before *Logout*.

This is a soft requirement because there may well be stories that depend on other stories being implemented first. For example, if we define *Login* without any forgotten password recovery, then clearly *Password Recovery* depends, to some extent, upon *Login*. Still, we try to separate the stories so that there is as little dependence as possible. This allows us to implement the stories in the order of business value.

- **N: Negotiable.** This is another reason why we don't write down all the details. We want those details to be negotiable between the developers and the business.

For example, the business might ask for a fancy drag-and-drop interface to some feature. The developers could recommend a simpler checkbox style by saying that it would be much less expensive to develop. Negotiations like that are important because it is one of the few ways that the business gains insight into ways of managing the cost of developing software.

- **V: Valuable.** The story must have clear and quantifiable value to the business.

Refactoring is *never* a story. Architecture is never a story. Code cleanup is never a story. A story is always something that the business values. Don't worry, we *will* deal with refactoring, architecture, and cleanup—but not with stories.

This usually means that a story will cut through all the layers of a system. It may involve a little GUI, a little middleware, some database work, etc. Think of a story as a thin vertical slice through the horizontal layers of the system.

Quantifying the business value can be informal. Some teams might simply use high/medium/low as their business value scale; others might try to use a ten-point scale. It doesn't matter what scale you use as long as you can differentiate between stories that differ significantly in value.

- **E: Estimable.** A user story must be concrete enough to allow the developers to estimate it.

A story such as *The System Must Be Fast* is not estimable because it is not closed; it's a background requirement that all stories must implement.

- **S: Small.** A user story should not be larger than one or two developers can implement in a single iteration.

We don't want a single story to dominate the whole team for an entire iteration. An iteration should contain about the same number of stories as there are developers on the team. If the team has 8 developers, then each iteration should contain about 6 to 12 stories. You don't want to get too hung up on this point, however; it's more a guideline than a rule.

- **T: Testable.** The business should be able to articulate tests that will prove that the story has been completed.

Typically, those tests will be written by QA, will be automated, and will be used to determine whether a story is complete. We'll have much more to say about this later. For now, just remember that a story has to be concrete enough to specify with tests.

This may seem to contradict **N** above. It doesn't, because we don't have to know the test at the time we write the story. All we need to know is that a test can be written at the appropriate time. So for example, even though I don't know all the details of the *Login* story, I *know* that it is testable because

Login is a concrete operation. On the other hand, a story like *Usable* is not testable. It's also not estimable. Indeed, the **E** and **T** go together pretty closely.

STORY ESTIMATION

There are a number of schemes for estimating stories. Most of them are variations on the old Wideband Delphi[5] approach.

One of the simplest is called *Flying Fingers*. Developers sit around a table, read a story, and discuss it with stakeholders if necessary. Then the developers put one hand behind their back, out of sight, and hold up the number of fingers that corresponds to the number of points they think the story deserves. Then someone counts one…two…three… and then all the fingers come flying out at once.

If everyone is holding the same number of fingers, or if the deviation is small and has an obvious mean, then that number is written on the story card, and the team moves on to the next story. If, however, there is substantial disagreement between the fingers, then the developers discuss the reasons why, and then repeat the process until agreement is reached.

A reasonable range for stories is *Shirt Sizes:* small, medium, and large. If you want to use all five fingers, go ahead. On the other hand, more than a handful of rankings is almost certainly absurd. Remember, we want to be accurate, but no more precise than necessary.

Planning Poker[6] is a similar technique, but it involves cards. There are many popular Planning Poker card decks out there. Most use some kind of Fibonacci series. One popular deck contains the cards: ?, 0, ½, 1, 2, 3, 5, 8, 13, 20, 40, 100, and ∞. If you use such a deck, my advice to you would be to remove most of those cards.

---

5. https://en.wikipedia.org/wiki/Wideband_delphi
6. Grenning, J. W. 2002. Planning Poker or how to avoid analysis paralysis while release planning. Accessed at https://wingman-sw.com/articles/planning-poker.

A benefit of the Fibonacci series is that it allows the team to estimate larger stories. For example, you could choose 1, 2, 3, 5, and 8, which gives you an 8X range in size.

You may also wish to include 0, ∞, and ?. In *Flying Fingers,* you can use thumbs down, thumbs up, and an open hand for these symbols. Zero means, "Too trivial to estimate." Be careful with those! You may wish to merge a few of them into a bigger story. Infinity (∞) represents too big to estimate, and therefore the story should be split. And (?) means you simply don't know, meaning that you'll need a *spike*.

Splitting, Merging, and Spiking

Merging stories is simple. You can clip the cards together and treat the merged stories as one. Just add up all the points. If any have zero points, use your best judgment in summing them. After all, fives zeros probably does not add up to zero.

Splitting stories is a bit more interesting because you need to maintain INVEST. As a simple example of splitting a story, consider *Login*. If we wanted to split it into smaller stories, we could create *Login with No Password, Login with Single Password Attempt, Allow Multiple Password Attempts,* and *Forgot Password*.

It is rare to find a story that cannot be split. This is especially true of those that are big enough to need splitting. Remember, it is the job of a programmer to split stories all the way down into individual lines of code. So splitting is almost always possible. The challenge is maintaining INVEST.

A *spike* is a meta-story, or rather, a story for estimating a story. It is called a *spike* because it often requires us to develop a long but very thin slice through all the layers of the system.

Let's say there's a story that you cannot estimate. Let's call it *Print PDF*. Why don't you know how to estimate it? Because you've never used the PDF library before and you aren't sure how it works. So you write a new story called *Estimate Print PDF*. Now you estimate *that* story, which is easier to estimate.

After all, you know what you'll have to do to figure out how the PDF library works. Both stories go in the deck.

In a future IPM, the stakeholders may decide to play the *Print PDF* card, but they can't because of the spike. They have to play the spike card instead. That will allow the developers to do the work necessary to estimate the original story, which can be implemented in a future iteration.

MANAGING THE ITERATION

The goal of each iteration is to produce data by getting stories done. The team should focus on stories rather than tasks within stories. It is far better to get 80% of the stories done than it is to get each story 80% done. Focus on driving the stories to completion.

As soon as the planning meeting ends, the programmers should choose the stories for which they will each individually be responsible. Some teams choose the first stories and leave the rest in a pile to be chosen later as stories are completed. Either way, stories are chosen by, and belong to, individual programmers.

Managers and leads will be tempted to assign stories to programmers. This should be avoided. It is far better to let the programmers negotiate amongst themselves.

For example:

Jerry (Journeyman): If nobody minds, I'll take Login *and* Logout. *It makes sense to do them together.*

Jasmine (Journeyman): I don't have a problem with that, but why don't you pair with Alphonse on the database part. He's been asking about our event-sourcing style, and Login *would be a gentle introduction. Alphonse?*

Alphonse (Apprentice): *That sounds great to me. Once I've seen that I should be able to work on* Withdraw.

Alexis (Lead programmer): *Why don't I take* Withdraw, *Alphonse. You can pair with me on that, too. Then you can take* Transfer.

Alphonse: *Aw, OK. That probably makes more sense. Small steps, right?*

Jasmine: *Right, Al. And that leaves* Deposit. *I'll take that one. Alexis, you and I should put our heads together on the UIs because they're likely similar. We might be able to share some code.*

In this example, you can see how the lead programmer guides the new, ambitious apprentice away from biting off more than he can chew, and how the team generally collaborates on choosing the stories.

QA and Acceptance Tests

If QA has not already begun to write the automated acceptance tests, they should start as soon as the IPM ends. The tests for stories that are scheduled for early completion should be done early. We don't want completed stories waiting for acceptance tests to be written.

Acceptance test writing should go quickly. We expect them to all be written before the midpoint of the iteration. If not all the acceptance tests are ready by the midpoint, then some of the developers should stop working on stories and start working on acceptance tests.

This will likely mean that not all the stories will be completed in this iteration, but a story cannot be completed without the acceptance tests anyway. Just be sure that the programmers working on a story are not also writing the acceptance tests for that story. If QA continues to miss the midpoint deadline, one iteration after another, then the ratio of QA engineers to developers is likely wrong.

After the midpoint, if all the acceptance tests are done, QA should be working on the tests for the next iteration. This is a bit speculative since the IPM hasn't happened yet, but the stakeholders can offer guidance about the stories most likely to be chosen.

Developers and QA should be communicating intensely about these tests. We don't want QA to simply "throw the tests over the wall" to the developers. Rather, they should be negotiating how the tests are structured and collaborating on writing them, even to the point of pairing together on the writing of them.

As the midpoint of the iteration approaches, the team should be trying to get stories done for the midpoint review. As the end of the iteration approaches, developers should be trying to get the remaining stories to pass their respective acceptance tests.

The definition of "done" is this: acceptance tests pass.

On the last day of the iteration, tough choices may be required regarding which stories will be completed and which will have to be abandoned. We do this so that we can reallocate effort to get as many stories done as possible. Again, we don't want to end the iteration with two half-done stories when we could have sacrificed one story in order to get the other one done.

This is not about going fast. This is about making concrete, measurable progress. This is about reliable data. When the acceptance tests for a story pass, that story is done. However, when a programmer says that a story is 90% done, we really don't know how close to done it is. So, the only thing we ever want to report on our velocity chart is stories that have passed their acceptance tests.

THE DEMO

The iteration ends with a brief demonstration of the new stories to the stakeholders. This meeting need be no more than an hour or two long, depending on the iteration size. The demo should include showing that all the acceptance tests run—including all *previous* acceptance tests—and all unit tests. It should also show off the newly added features. It is best if the stakeholders themselves operate the system so that the developers aren't tempted to hide things that don't work.

VELOCITY

The last act of the iteration is to update the velocity and burn-down charts. Only the points for stories that have passed their acceptance tests are recorded on these charts. After several iterations, both of these charts will begin to show a slope. The burn-down slope predicts the date for the next major milestone. The velocity slope tells us how well the team is being managed.

The velocity slope will be pretty noisy, especially during early iterations, as the team is still figuring out the basics of the project. But after the first few iterations, the noise should reduce to a level that allows an average velocity to become apparent.

We expect that after the first few iterations, the slope will be zero—that is, horizontal. We don't expect the team to be speeding up or slowing down over long periods.

Rising Velocity

If we see a positive slope, it likely does *not* mean that the team is actually going faster. Rather, it probably means that the project manager is putting pressure on the team to go faster. As that pressure builds, the team will unconsciously shift the value of their estimates to make it appear that they are going faster.

This is simple inflation. The points are a currency, and the team is devaluing them under external pressure. Come back to that team next year, and they'll be getting millions of points done per iteration. The lesson here is that velocity is a *measurement* not an objective. It's control theory 101: don't put pressure on the thing you are measuring.

The purpose of estimating the iteration during the IPM is simply so that the stakeholders know how many stories *might* get done. This helps the stakeholders choose the stories and helps them to plan. But that estimate is not a promise, and the team has not failed if the actual velocity is lower.

Remember, the only failing iteration is an iteration that fails to produce data.

Falling Velocity

If the velocity chart shows a consistent negative slope, then the most likely cause is the quality of the code. The team is likely not refactoring enough and they are probably allowing the code to rot. One reason that teams fail to refactor enough is that they don't write enough unit tests, so they fear that refactoring will break something that used to work. Managing this fear of change is a major goal of team management, and it all comes down to the testing discipline. We'll have much more to say about that later.

As velocity falls, pressure on the team builds. This causes the points to inflate. That inflation can hide the falling velocity.

The Golden Story

One way to avoid inflation is to constantly compare story estimates back to the original *Golden Story*, the standard against which other stories will be measured. Remember that *Login* was our original *Golden Story*, and it was estimated as 3. If a new story such as *Fix Spelling Error in Menu Item* has an estimate of 10, you know that some inflationary force is at work.

SMALL RELEASES

The practice of *Small Releases* suggests that a development team should release their software as often as possible. Back in the late '90s, in the early days of Agile, we thought that this meant a release every "month or two." Nowadays, however, we've set the goal to be much, much, shorter. Indeed, we've made it infinitely shorter. The new goal, of course, is *Continuous Delivery:* the practice of releasing the code to production after every change.

This description could be misleading because the term *Continuous Delivery* makes it seem like the cycle that we want to shorten is only the *delivery* cycle. Actually, we want to shorten *every* cycle.

Unfortunately, there is a significant historical inertia to shortening cycles. That inertia has to do with the way we managed our source code back in the olden days.

A Brief History of Source Code Control

The story of source code control is the story of cycles and their sizes. It begins in the 1950s and '60s when source code was kept in the holes punched in bits of paper (Figure 3.3).

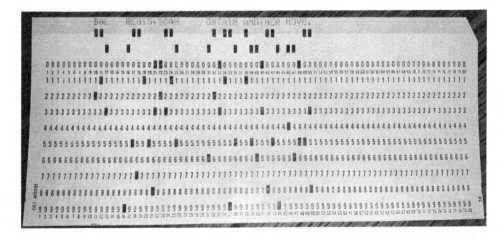

Figure 3.3 A punched card

Many of us used punched cards in those days. A card held 80 characters and represented one line of a program. The program itself was a deck of such cards, typically held together with a rubber band and kept in a box (Figure 3.4).

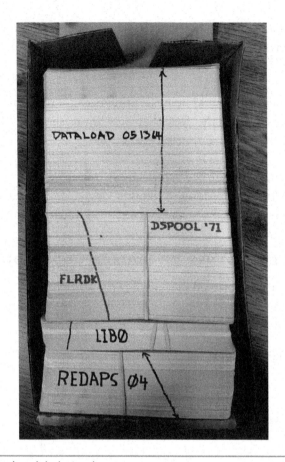

Figure 3.4 Punched card decks in a box

The owner of that program kept the deck in a drawer or a cabinet. If someone wanted to check out the source code, he *literally* checked out the source code from the drawer or cabinet, with the permission of the owner.

If you had the source code checked out, you were the only one who could change that source code because you had *physical* possession of it. Nobody else could touch it. When you were done, you gave the deck back to the owner, who put it back in the drawer or cabinet.

The cycle time for that program was the amount of time that a programmer kept possession of it. That time could be days, weeks, or months.

TAPES

In the 1970s, we gradually transitioned to keeping our source code in card images stored on magnetic tape. Magnetic tapes could hold a large number of source code modules, and they were easy to duplicate. The procedure for editing a module was as follows.

1. Get the master tape from the master rack.
2. Copy the modules you want to edit from the master tape to a work tape.
3. Put the master tape back so other people could access other modules.
4. Put a colored pin in the checkout board next to the name of the modules you want to edit. (I was blue, my boss was red, and the other programmer on my team was yellow. Yes, eventually we ran out of colors.)
5. Edit, compile, and test using the work tape.
6. Get the master tape again.
7. Copy the changed modules from the work tape to a new copy of the master tape.
8. Put the new master in the rack.
9. Remove your pin from the board.

Once again, the cycle time was the time your pin was present on the board. This could be hours, days, or even weeks. So long as your pins were in the checkout board, nobody else was supposed to touch the modules you had pinned.

Of course, those modules were still on the master tape, and in a pinch, someone else could violate the rules and edit the modules. So the pins were a convention, not a physical barrier.

DISKS AND SCCS

In the '80s, we moved our source code to disk. At first, we continued to use the pins in the checkout board; then, some real source code control tools started to appear. The first I remember was Source Code Control System (SCCS). SCCS behaved just like the checkout board. You locked a module on disk, preventing anyone else from editing it. This kind of lock is called a *pessimistic lock*. Again, the cycle time was the length of the lock. It could be hours, days, or months.

SCCS gave way to Revision Control System (RCS), which gave way to Concurrent Versions System (CVS), all of which used one form or another of pessimistic lock. So the cycle time remained long. However, disks are a much more convenient medium of storage than tapes. The process of copying modules from master to work tapes tempted us to keep those modules large. Disks, on the other hand, allowed us to shrink the size of our modules drastically. There simply was no penalty for having many small modules as opposed to a few large ones. This effectively shortened the cycle time simply because the amount of time you would keep a small module checked out was relatively small.

The problem was that changes to a system usually required changes to many modules. To the extent that the system was deeply coupled, the effective checkout time was still long. Some of us learned to decouple our modules to shorten that checkout time. Most, however, did not.

SUBVERSION

Then came Subversion (SVN). This tool offered *optimistic locks*. An optimistic lock is not really a lock at all. One developer could check out a module at the same time that another had it checked out. The tool kept track of this and automatically merged changes into the modules. If the tool detected a conflict (i.e., the two developers changed the same lines of code) it forced the programmer to resolve the conflict before allowing the checkin.

This drastically shortened the cycle time to the time required to edit, compile, and test a series of small changes. Coupling was still an issue. A tightly coupled system maintained long cycle times because many modules had to be changed in unison. But a loosely coupled system could be cycled much more quickly. Checkout time was no longer the limiting factor.

GIT AND TESTS

Nowadays we use Git. Checkout time using Git has shrunk to zero. The concept doesn't exist. Rather, any alteration to a module can be committed at any time. Conflicts among these commits are resolved as and when the programmers desire. Tiny decoupled modules and rapid commit frequency result in cycle times that can be as small as minutes. Add to this the ability to create a comprehensive, fast-running test suite that tests almost *everything,* and you have the makings of *Continuous Delivery.*

Historical Inertia

Unfortunately, it is difficult for organizations to shake off the behaviors of the past. The cycle time of days, weeks, and months is deeply ingrained in the culture of many teams and has spread to QA, to management, and to the expectations of the stakeholders. From the vantage of such a culture, the notion of *Continuous Delivery* can seem ludicrous.

Small Releases

Agile attempts to break that historical inertia by driving the team to shorter and shorter release cycles. If you are releasing every six months, try every three months, then try every month, then try every week. Keep shortening the release cycle in an asymptotic approach to zero.

To do this, the organization will need to break the coupling between release and deployment. The term "release" means that the software is technically ready to be deployed. The decision to deploy becomes solely a business decision.

You may have noticed that this is the same language we used to describe iterations. Iterations are technically deployable. If our iterations are two weeks long, but we want to release more often than that, we'll have to shorten our iterations.

Can iterations be shortened asymptotically toward zero? Yes, they can. But that's a topic for another section.

ACCEPTANCE TESTS

The practice of Acceptance Tests is one of the least understood, least used, and most confused of all the Agile practices. This is strange because the underlying idea is remarkably simple: *Requirements should be specified by the business.*

The problem, of course, is the meaning of the word: *specify.* Many businesses would like that word to mean that they can wave their hands around in the air and describe the desired behavior in vague and fluffy terms. They want the developers to figure out all the little details. Many programmers would like the business to define *precisely* what the system should do, right down to the coordinates and values of each individual pixel.

Something in the middle of these two extremes is necessary.

So what is a specification? A specification is, by its very nature, *a test.* For example:

> *When the user enters a valid username and password, and then clicks "login," the system will present the "Welcome" page.*

This is obviously a specification. It is also obviously a test.

It should also be obvious that this test could be automated. There is no reason that a computer could not verify that the specification has been met.

This is the practice of Acceptance Tests. The practice says that, to the degree practicable, the requirements of the system should be written as automated tests.

But wait! Who writes these automated tests? The first paragraph in this section answers that question: *Requirements should be specified by the business.* So the business should write the automated tests. Right?

But wait! Automated tests have to be written in some kind of formal executable language. That sounds like a job for programmers. So programmers should write the automated tests, right?

But wait! If programmers write the tests, they won't be written from the business' point of view. They'll be technical tests full of details that only programmers understand. They won't reflect the item's business value. So the business should write the automated tests. Right?

But wait! If the business writes the automated tests then they'll be written in a way that doesn't match the technology we're using. The programmers will just have to rewrite them, right?

You can see why this practice has been so confusing for so many people.

TOOLS AND METHODOLOGIES

It's worse than that because the practice has been inundated with tools and methodologies.

In an attempt to make it easier for business people to write automated tests, programmers have written a plethora of tools to "help." These tools include things like FitNesse, JBehave, SpecFlow, and Cucumber. Each of these tools creates a formalism that attempts to separate the technical and business sides of an automated test. The working hypothesis is that the business can write the business side of the automated tests, and the programmers can write the glue code that binds those tests to the system being tested.

This seems like a good idea, and the tools do a decent job of this separation. Yet businesses have been reluctant to engage. The businesspeople who are responsible for specification are wary of formal languages. They typically want to use a human language, like English, to write their specifications.

In response to this reluctance, programmers have stepped in and written the acceptance tests for the businesspeople, in the hopes that the businesspeople will at least *read* the formal documents. But this hasn't worked out all that well either, because the businesspeople don't like the formal languages. They'd rather either see the system actually work, or better yet, delegate the job of verification to QA.

BEHAVIOR-DRIVEN DEVELOPMENT

After the turn of the millennium, Dan North began working on a redefinition of TDD that he called *Behavior-Driven Development* (BDD). His goal was to remove the techie jargon from the tests and make the tests appear more like specifications that businesspeople would appreciate.

At first, this was just another attempt at formalizing the language of testing, in this case using three special adverbs: *Given, When,* and *Then.* Several tools were created or modified to support this language. Among them are JBehave, Cucumber, and FitNesse. But over time, the emphasis changed from tools and tests to requirements and specification.

The proponents of BDD suggest that businesses can derive great value by specifying their systems in a formal scenario-based language like Given-When-Then, regardless of whether they actually automate those requirements as tests.

This relieves the businesspeople from conforming to the technical requirements involved with writing truly executable tests, while at the same time allowing them to be formal and precise.

THE PRACTICE

Despite all the controversy and confusion described above, the practice of *Acceptance Testing* is actually quite simple. The business writes formal tests describing the behavior of each user story, and developers automate those tests.

The tests are written by business analysts and QA before the first half of the iteration in which the stories they test are to be developed. The developers integrate those tests into the continuous build. Those tests become the *Definition of Done* for the stories in the iteration. A story is not specified until its acceptance test is written. A story is not complete until its acceptance test passes.

Business Analysts and QA

Acceptance tests are a collaborative effort between business analysts, QA, and the developers. Business analysts specify the happy paths. That's because they have enough to do in their role of communicating between the programmers and the stakeholders.

QA's role is to write the unhappy paths. There are a lot more of them than there are of the former. QA folks are hired for their ability to figure out how to break the system. They are deeply technical people who can foresee all the strange and bizarre things that users are going to do to the system. They also know the minds of programmers and understand how to probe all their lazy streaks.

And, of course, the developers work with QA and business analysts to ensure that the tests make sense from a technical point of view.

QA

This, of course, completely changes the role of QA. Rather than acting as testers on the back end of the project, they become specifiers operating at the front end of the project. Instead of supplying late feedback about errors and omissions, they are providing early input to the development team to prevent those errors and omissions.

This puts a much greater burden upon QA. QA must now ensure quality by injecting it into the start of each iteration, rather than measuring lack of compliance at the end. However, the responsibility of QA is not diminished in any way; they determine whether the system is deployable.

Losing the Tests at the End

Moving QA to the beginning and automating the tests solves another huge problem. When QA operates manually at the end, they are the bottleneck. They must finish their work before the system can be deployed. Impatient managers and stakeholders lean on QA to finish up so that the system can be deployed.

When QA comes at the end, all upstream delays fall on QA. If the developers are late delivering to QA, does the delivery date change? Often the delivery date was chosen for very good business reasons, and delaying it would be costly, or even catastrophic. QA is left holding the bag.

How should QA test the system when they have no time left in the schedule to test it? How can QA go faster? That's easy: don't test everything. Just test the things that changed. Do an impact analysis based on new and changed features, and only test the impacted things. Don't waste time testing things that haven't changed.

So you lose the tests. Under pressure, QA simply bypasses all the regression tests. They hope that they can run them next time. Often, "next time" never comes.

The QA Disease

However, that's not the worst problem that happens because QA is at the end of the process. When QA is at the end, how does the organization know they are doing their jobs well? By their defect count, of course. If QA is finding lots of defects, they are clearly doing their job well. QA managers can tout the number of defects found as clear evidence that they are performing their function.

Thus, defects are considered a *good thing*.

Who else can benefit from defects? There's a saying among older programmers: "I can meet any deadline you set for me, as long as the software doesn't have to work properly." So who else benefits from defects? Developers who need to meet schedule deadlines.

No word needs to be spoken. No agreement needs to be written. But both sides understand that they benefit from defects. A black market economy of defects emerges. This disease permeates many organizations, and if it's not terminal, it's certainly debilitating.

Developers Are the Testers

These problems are all cured by the practice of *Acceptance Tests*. QA writes the acceptance tests for the stories in an iteration. *But QA does not run those tests*. It's not QA's job to verify that the system passes the tests. Whose job is it? The programmers', of course!

It is the programmers' job to run the tests. It is the programmers' job to make sure that their code passes all the tests. So of course, the programmers must run those tests. Running those tests is the only way for programmers to determine whether their stories are done.

Continuous Build

Indeed, the programmers will automate that process[7] by setting up a Continuous Build server. This server will simply run all the tests in the system, including all unit tests and all acceptance tests, every time any programmer checks in a module. We'll have more to say about that when we talk about Continuous Integration.

WHOLE TEAM

The practice of *Whole Team* was initially called *On-Site Customer*. The idea was that the shorter the distance between the users and the programmers, the better the communication, and the faster and more accurate the development. The *customer* was a metaphor for someone, or some group, who understood the needs of the users, and who was co-located with the development team. Ideally, the customer sat in the same room with the team.

---

7. Because automating things is what programmers do!

In Scrum, the customer is called the *Product Owner*. This is the person (or group) who chooses stories, sets priorities, and provides immediate feedback.

The practice was renamed *Whole Team* in order to make it clear that a development team was not simply a customer/programmer dyad. Instead, a development team is composed of many roles including managers, testers, technical writers, etc. The goal of the practice is to minimize the physical distance between these roles. Ideally, all members of the team sit together in the same room.

There can be little doubt that putting the entire team into a single room maximizes the efficiency of that team. The individuals can communicate rapidly and with a minimum of formality. Questions can be asked and answered within seconds. The experts who know the answers are always near.

Moreover, there is a huge opportunity for serendipity. An on-site customer may look over and see something on a programmer's or tester's screen that doesn't look right. A tester may overhear a programming pair talking about a requirement and realize that they've come to the wrong conclusion. This kind of accidental synergy should not be undervalued. When the Whole Team sits together in the same space, magic can happen.

Notice that this practice is counted as a *business* practice, and not a team practice. That's because the primary advantages of the Whole Team practice accrue to the business.

When teams are co-located, the business runs much more smoothly.

Co-Location

In the early 2000s, I helped several organizations adopt Agile methods. In our preliminary visits, before the active coaching began, we asked our customers to set up team rooms and co-locate the teams. More than once, the customer reported that the efficiency of the teams increased dramatically simply because of the co-location.

Co-Location Alternatives

In the 1990s, the internet made it feasible to take advantage of vast pools of programming labor in countries where the cost of that labor was very low. The temptation to use this labor was overwhelming. Accountants did the math, and their eyes sparkled with the savings they believed they could achieve.

This dream didn't work out quite as well as everyone hoped. It turns out that the ability to send megabits of source code around the world is not quite the same as having a team of co-located customers and programmers. The distances in terms of miles, time zones, language, and culture were still huge. Miscommunication was rampant. Quality was severely limited. Rework soared.[8]

In the years since, the technology has improved somewhat. Data throughput rates now allow regular video chat and screen-sharing sessions. Two developers located on opposite sides of the world can now pair on the same code almost as though they were sitting next to each other—almost. Of course, these advances don't solve the time-zone, language, and culture issues; but electronic face-to-face coding is certainly preferable to emailing source code back and forth.

Can an Agile team work this way? I've heard that it is possible. I've never seen it done successfully. Perhaps you have.

Working Remotely from Home

The improvement in internet bandwidth has also made it much easier for people to work from home. In this case, the language, time zone, and culture aren't significant issues. What's more, there is no trans-ocean communications lag. Team meetings can occur almost as if co-located and in sync with everyone's circadian rhythms.

---

8. These are my own impressions based upon talking with folks who experienced the issues directly. I have no actual data to present. Caveat emptor.

Don't get me wrong. When team members work from home, there is still a significant loss of nonverbal communication. Serendipitous conversations are much rarer. No matter how electronically connected the team is, they are still not together in the same space. This puts the people working from home at a distinct disadvantage. There are always conversations and impromptu meetings that they miss. Despite the vast data bandwidth they may enjoy, they are still communicating through a peephole compared to those who are co-located.

A team that is mostly co-located but has a member or two who work from home one or two days per week will likely not notice any significant impediment, especially if they have invested in some good, high-bandwidth remote-communication tools.

On the other hand, a team composed of people who work almost entirely from home will never work as well as a team that is co-located.

Don't get me wrong. In the early '90s, my partner Jim Newkirk and I successfully managed a team that had no co-location at all. Everyone worked entirely from home. We met in person twice per year at most, and some of us lived in different time zones. On the other hand, we all spoke the same language, shared the same culture, and our time zones were never more than two hours apart. We made it work. We made it work very well. But it would have worked even better if we'd been together in the same room.

CONCLUSION

At the Snowbird meeting in 2000, Kent Beck said that one of our goals was to heal the divide between business and development. The business-facing practices play a big role in satisfying that goal. By following these practices, business and development have a simple and unambiguous way to communicate. That communication breeds trust.

TEAM 4 PRACTICES

The middle band within Ron Jeffries' Circle of Life consists of the Team Practices of Agile. These practices govern the relationship of the team members with one another and with the product they are creating. The practices we will discuss are Metaphor, Sustainable Pace, Collective Ownership, and Continuous Integration.

Then we'll talk briefly about so-called *Standup Meetings*.

METAPHOR

In the years just before and after the signing of the Agile Manifesto, the *Metaphor* practice was something of an embarrassment for us because we couldn't describe it. We knew it was important, and we could point to some successful examples. But we were unable to effectively articulate what we meant. In several of our talks, lectures, or classes, we simply bailed out and said things like, "You'll know it when you see it."

The idea is that in order for the team to communicate effectively, they require a constrained and disciplined vocabulary of terms and concepts. Kent Beck called this a *Metaphor* because it related his projects to something else about which the teams had common knowledge.

Beck's primary example was the Metaphor used by the Chrysler payroll project.[1] He related the production of a paycheck to an assembly line. The paychecks would move from station to station getting "parts" added to them. A blank check might move to the ID station to get the employee's identification added. Then it might move to the pay station to get the gross pay added. Next it might move to the federal tax station, and then the FICA station, and then the Medicare station... You get the idea.

The programmers and customers could pretty easily apply this metaphor to the process of building a paycheck. It gave them a vocabulary to use when talking about the system.

But metaphors often go wrong.

---

1. https://en.wikipedia.org/wiki/Chrysler_Comprehensive_Compensation_System

For example, in the late '80s, I worked on a project that measured the quality of T1 communication networks. We downloaded error counts from the endpoints of each T1 line. Those error counts were collected into 30-minute time slices. We considered those slices to be raw data that needed to be cooked. What cooks slices? A *toaster*. And thus began the *bread* metaphor. We had slices, loaves, crumbs, etc.

This vocabulary worked well for the programmers. We were able to talk with each other about raw and toasted slices, loaves, etc. On the other hand, the managers and customers who overheard us would walk out of the room shaking their heads. To them we appeared to be talking nonsense.

As a much worse example, in the early '70s I worked on a time-sharing system that swapped applications in and out of limited memory space. During the time that an application occupied memory, it would load up a buffer of text to be sent out to a slow teletype. When that buffer was full, the application would be put to sleep and swapped out to disk while the buffers slowly emptied. We called those buffers garbage trucks, running back and forth between the producer of the garbage and the dump.

We thought this was clever. Our use of garbage, as a metaphor, made us giggle. In effect, we were saying that our customers were garbage merchants. As effective as the metaphor was for our communication, it was disrespectful to those who were paying us. We never shared it with them.

These examples show both the advantages and disadvantages of the *Metaphor* idea. A metaphor can provide a vocabulary that allows the team to communicate efficiently. On the other hand, some metaphors are silly to the point of being offensive to the customer.

DOMAIN-DRIVEN DESIGN

In his groundbreaking book *Domain-Driven Design*,[2] Eric Evans solved the metaphor problem and finally erased our embarrassment. In that book, he coined the term *Ubiquitous Language*, which is the name that should have

---

2. Evans, E. 2003. *Domain-Driven Design: Tackling Complexity in the Heart of Software*. Boston, MA: Addison-Wesley.

been given to the *Metaphor* practice. What the team needs is a model of the problem domain, which is described by a vocabulary that everyone agrees on. And I mean *everyone*—the programmers, QA, managers, customers, users... *everyone*.

In the 1970s, Tom DeMarco called such models *Data Dictionaries*.[3] They were simple representations of the data manipulated by the application and the processes that manipulated that data. Evans greatly amplified that simple idea into a discipline of modeling the domain. Both DeMarco and Evans use those models as vehicles to communicate with all of the stakeholders.

As a simple example, I recently wrote a video game called SpaceWar. The data elements were things like Ship, Klingon, Romulan, Shot, Hit, Explosion, Base, Transport, etc. I was careful to isolate each of these concepts into their own modules and to use those names exclusively throughout the application. Those names were my Ubiquitous Language.

The Ubiquitous Language is used in all parts of the project. The business uses it. The developers use it. QA uses it. Ops/Devops use it. Even the customers use those parts of it that are appropriate. It supports the business case, the requirements, the design, the architecture, and the acceptance tests. It is a thread of consistency that interconnects the entire project during every phase of its lifecycle.[4]

SUSTAINABLE PACE

"The race is not to the swift..."

— Ecclesiastes 9:11

"...But he who endures to the end will be saved."

— Matthew 24:13

---

3. DeMarco, T. 1979. *Structured Analysis and System Specification*. Upper Saddle River, NJ: Yourdon Press.

4. "It's an energy field created by all living things. It surrounds us and penetrates us. It binds the galaxy together." Lucas, G. 1979. *Star Wars: Episode IV—A New Hope*. Lucasfilm.

On the seventh day, God rested. God later made it a commandment to rest on the seventh day. Apparently even God needs to run at a Sustainable Pace.

In the early '70s, at the tender age of 18, my high school buddies and I were hired as new programmers working on a *critically important* project. Our *managers* had set *deadlines*. Those deadlines were *absolute*. Our efforts were *important!* We were *critical cogs* in the machinery of the organization. *We were important!*

It's good to be 18, isn't it?

We, young men right out of high school, pulled out all the stops. We worked hours and hours and hours, for months and months and months. Our weekly average was over 60 hours. There were weeks that peaked above 80 hours. We pulled dozens of all-nighters!

And we *prided* ourselves on all that overtime. We were *real* programmers. We were *dedicated*. We were *valuable*. Because we were *single-handedly saving* a project that was *important*. We. Were. *Programmers*.

And then we burned out—*hard*. So hard that we quit *en masse*. We stormed out of there, leaving the company holding a barely functioning time-share system without any competent programmers to support it. *That'll show 'em!*

It's good to be 18 and angry, isn't it?

Don't worry, the company muddled through. It turned out that we were not the only competent programmers there. There were folks there who had carefully worked 40 hours per week. Folks whom we had disparaged as undedicated and lazy in our private late-night programming orgies. Those folks quietly picked up the reins and maintained the system just fine. And, I daresay, they were happy to be rid of us angry, noisy kids.

OVERTIME

You'd think that I would have learned my lesson from that experience. But, of course, I did not. Over the next 20 years, I continued to work long hours for my employers. I continued to fall for the *important project* meme. Oh, I didn't work the crazy hours I worked when I was 18. My average weekly hours dropped to more like 50. All-nighters became pretty rare—but, as we shall see, not entirely absent.

As I matured, I realized that my worst technical mistakes were made during those periods of frenetic late-night energy. I realized that those mistakes were huge impediments that I had to constantly work around during my truly wakeful hours.

Then came the event that made me reconsider my ways. My future business partner, Jim Newkirk, and I were pulling an all-nighter. Sometime around 2 a.m., we were trying to figure out how to get a piece of data from a low-level part of our system to another part that was much higher up the execution chain. Returning this data up the stack was not an option.

We had built a "mail" transport system within our product. We used it to send information *between* processes. We suddenly realized, at 2 a.m., with caffeine roaring through our veins and all our faculties operating at peak efficiency, that we could have the low-level part of the process mail that piece of data to itself where the high-level part could fetch it.

Even today, more than three decades later, whenever Jim and I want to describe someone else's unfortunate decision, we say: "Uh-oh. They just mailed it to themselves."

I won't bore you with all the horrible, nitty-gritty details about why that decision was so awful. Suffice it to say, it cost us many times the effort that we thought we were saving. And of course, the solution became too entrenched to reverse, so we were stuck with it.[5]

---

5. This was a decade before I would learn about TDD. Had Jim and I been practicing TDD back then, we could have easily backed out that change.

MARATHON

That was the moment that I learned that a software project is a marathon, not a sprint, nor a sequence of sprints. In order to win, you must pace yourself. If you leap out of the blocks and run at full speed, you'll run out of energy long before you cross the finish line.

Thus, you must run at a pace that you can sustain over the long haul. You must run at a *Sustainable Pace*. If you try to run faster than the pace you can sustain, you will have to slow down and rest before you reach the finish line, and your average speed will be slower than the Sustainable Pace. When you are close to the finish line, if you have a bit of spare energy, you can sprint. But you must not sprint before that.

Managers may ask you to run faster than you should. You must not comply. It is your job to husband your resources to ensure that you endure to the end.

DEDICATION

Working overtime is not a way to show your dedication to your employer. What it shows is that you are a bad planner, that you agree to deadlines to which you shouldn't agree, that you make promises you shouldn't make, that you are a manipulable laborer and not a professional.

This is not to say that all overtime is bad, nor that you should never work overtime. There are extenuating circumstances for which the only option is to work overtime. But they should be extremely rare. And you must be very *aware* that the cost of that overtime will likely be greater than the time you save on the schedule.

That all-nighter that I pulled with Jim all those decades ago was not the last all-nighter I was to pull—it was the second to last. The last all-nighter I pulled was one of those extenuating circumstances over which I had no control.

The year was 1995. My first book was scheduled to go to press the next day, and I was on the hook to deliver page proofs. It was 6 p.m. and I had them all ready to go. All I needed to do was to FTP them to my publisher.

But then, by sheer accident, I stumbled across a way to *double* the resolution of the hundreds of diagrams in that book. Jim and Jennifer were helping me get the page proofs ready, and we were just about to execute the FTP when I showed an example of the improved resolution to them.

We all looked at each other, heaved a great sigh, and Jim said, "We have to redo them all." It wasn't a question. It was a statement of fact. The three of us looked at each other, at the clock, back at each other, and then we buckled down and got to work.

But when we were done with that all-nighter, we were *done*. The book shipped. And we slept.

SLEEP

The most precious ingredient in the life of a programmer is sufficient sleep. I do well on seven hours. I can tolerate a day or two of six hours. Anything less, and my productivity plummets. Make sure you know how many hours of sleep your body needs, and then prioritize those hours. Those hours will more than pay themselves back. My rule of thumb is that the first hour of insufficient sleep costs me two hours of daytime work. The second hour of insufficient sleep costs me another four hours of productive work. And, of course, there's no productive work at all if I'm three hours behind on my sleep.

COLLECTIVE OWNERSHIP

No one owns the code in an Agile project. The code is owned by the team as a whole. Any member of the team can check out and improve any module in the project at any time. The team owns the code *collectively*.

I learned *Collective Ownership* early in my career while working at Teradyne. We worked on a large system composed of fifty thousand lines of code partitioned into several hundred modules. Yet no one on the team owned any of those modules. We all strove to learn and improve all of those modules. Oh, some of us were more familiar with certain parts of the code than others, but we sought to spread rather than concentrate that experience.

That system was an early distributed network. There was a central computer that communicated with several dozen satellite computers that were distributed across the country. These computers communicated over 300-baud modem lines. There was no division between the programmers who worked on the central computer and the satellite computers. We all worked on the software for both of them.

These two computers had very different architectures. One was similar to a PDP-8 except that it had an 18-bit word. It had 256K of RAM and was loaded from magnetic tape cartridges. The other was a 8085 8-bit microprocessor with 32K of RAM and 32K of ROM.

We programmed these in assembler. The two machines had very different assembly languages and very different development environments. We all worked with both with equal comfort.

Collective Ownership does not mean that you cannot specialize. As systems grow in complexity, specialization becomes an absolute necessity. There are systems that simply cannot be understood in both entirety and detail. However, even as you specialize, you must also generalize. Divide your work between your specialty and other areas of the code. Maintain your ability to work outside of your specialty.

When a team practices *Collective Ownership*, knowledge becomes distributed across the team. Each team member gains a better understanding of the boundaries between modules and of the overall way that the system works. This drastically improves the ability of the team to communicate and make decisions.

In my rather long career, I have seen a few companies that practiced the opposite of *Collective Ownership*. Each programmer owned their own modules, and no one else was allowed to touch them. These were grossly dysfunctional teams who were constantly involved in finger pointing and miscommunication. All progress in a module would stop when the author was not at work. No one else dared to work on something owned by someone else.

THE X FILES

One particularly maladroit case was the company X, which built high-end printers. In the 1990s, the company was transitioning from a predominant hardware focus to an integrated hardware and software focus. They realized that they could cut their manufacturing costs significantly if they used software to control the internal operation of their machines.

However, the hardware focus was deeply ingrained, so the software groups were divided along the same lines as the hardware. The hardware teams were organized by device: there were respective hardware teams for the feeder, printer, stacker, stapler, etc. The software was organized according to the same devices. One team wrote the control software for the feeder, another team wrote the software for the stapler, and so forth.

In X, your political clout depended on the device you worked on. Since X was a printer company, the printer device was the most prestigious. The hardware engineers who worked on the printer had to come up through the ranks to get there. The stapler guys were nobodies.

Oddly, this same political ranking system applied to the software teams. The developers writing the stacker code were politically impotent; but if a printer developer spoke in a meeting, everyone else listened closely. Because of this political division, no one shared their code. The key to the printer team's political clout was locked up in the printer code. So the printer code stayed locked up, too. Nobody outside that team could see it.

The problems this caused were legion. There are the obvious communication difficulties when you can't inspect the code you are using. There is also the inevitable finger pointing and backstabbing.

But worse than that was the sheer, ridiculous duplication. It turns out that the control software for a feeder, printer, stacker, and stapler aren't that different. They all had to control motors, relays, solenoids, and clutches based upon external inputs and internal sensors. The basic internal structure of these modules was the same. And yet, because of all the political safeguarding, each team had to invent their own wheels independently.

Even more important, the very idea that the software should be divided along hardware lines was absurd. The software system did not need a feeder controller that was independent of the printer controller.

The waste of human resources, not to mention the emotional angst and adversarial posturing, led to a very uncomfortable environment. I believe that this environment was instrumental, at least in part, to their eventual downfall.

CONTINUOUS INTEGRATION

In the early days of Agile, the practice of *Continuous Integration* meant that developers checked in their source code changes and merged them with the main line every "couple of hours."[6] All unit tests and acceptance tests kept passing. No feature branches remained unintegrated. Any changes that should not be active when deployed were dealt with by using toggles.

In the year 2000, at one of our XP Immersion classes, a student got caught in a classic trap. These immersion classes were intense. We shortened the cycles down to single-day iterations. The Continuous Integration cycle was down to 15 to 30 minutes.

The student in question was working in a team of six developers, five of whom were checking in more frequently than he was. (He was not pairing for some reason—go figure.) Unfortunately, this student had kept his code unintegrated for over an hour.

---

6. Beck, K. 2000. *Extreme Programming Explained: Embrace Change*. Boston, MA: Addison-Wesley, p. 97.

When he finally tried to check in and integrate his changes, he found that so many other changes had accumulated that the merge took him a long time to get working. While he was struggling with that merge, the other programmers continued to make 15-minute checkins. When he finally got his merge working and tried to check in his code, he found he had another merge to do.

He was so frustrated by this that he stood up in the middle of class and loudly proclaimed, "XP doesn't work." Then he stormed out of the classroom and went to the hotel bar.

And then a miracle happened. The pair partner that he had rejected went after him to talk him down. The other two pairs reprioritized their work, finished the merge, and got the project back on track. Thirty minutes later the student, now much calmer, came back in the room, apologized, and resumed his work—including pairing. He subsequently became an enthusiastic advocate for Agile development.

The point is that Continuous Integration only works if you integrate continuously.

THEN CAME CONTINUOUS BUILD

In 2001, ThoughtWorks changed the game significantly. They created *CruiseControl*,[7] the first *continuous build* tool. I remember Mike Two[8] giving a late-night lecture about this at a 2001 XP Immersion. There's no recording of that speech, but the story went something like this:

> *CruiseControl allows the checkin time to shrink down to a few minutes. Even the most minor change is quickly integrated into the mainline. CruiseControl watches the source code control system and kicks off a build every time any change is checked in. As part of the build, CruiseControl runs the majority of the automated tests for the system and then sends email to everyone on the team with the results.*
>
> *"Bob, broke the build."*

---

7. https://en.wikipedia.org/wiki/CruiseControl
8. http://wiki.c2.com/?MikeTwo

We implemented a simple rule about breaking the build. On the day that you break the build, you have to wear a shirt that says, "I broke the build"—and no one ever washes that shirt.

Since those days, many other continuous build tools have been created. They include tools like *Jenkins* (or is it *Hudson?*), *Bamboo*, and *TeamCity*. These tools allow the time between integrations to shrink to a minimum. Kent's original "couple of hours" has been replaced by "a few minutes." Continuous Integration has become Continuous Checkin.

THE CONTINUOUS BUILD DISCIPLINE

The continuous build should *never* break. That's because, in order to avoid wearing Mike Two's dirty shirt, each programmer runs all acceptance tests and all unit tests before they check in their code. (Duh!) So if the build breaks, something very strange has happened.

Mike Two addressed this issue in his lecture, too. He described the calendar that they put in a prominent position on the wall of their team room. It was one of those large posters that had a square for every day of the year.

In any day where the build failed, even once, they placed a red dot. In any day where the build never failed, they placed a green dot. Just that simple visual was enough to transform a calendar of mostly red dots into a calendar of mostly green dots within a month or two.

Stop the Presses

Again: The continuous build should never break. A broken build is a *Stop the Presses* event. I want sirens going off. I want a big red light spinning in the CEO's office. A broken build is a *Big Effing Deal*. I want all the programmers to stop what they are doing and rally around the build to get it passing again. The mantra of the team must be *The Build Never Breaks*.

The Cost of Cheating

There have been teams who, under the pressure of a deadline, have allowed the continuous build to remain in a failed state. This is a suicidal move. What happens is that everyone gets tired of the continuous barrage of failure emails from the continuous build server, so they remove the failing tests with the promise that they'll go back and fix them "later."

Of course, this causes the continuous build server to start sending success emails again. Everyone relaxes. The build is passing. And everyone forgets about the pile of failing tests that they set aside to be fixed "later." And so a broken system gets deployed.

STANDUP MEETINGS

Over the years, there has been a great deal of confusion about "The Daily Scrum" or the "Standup Meeting." Let me cut through all that confusion now.

The following are true of the Standup Meeting:

- This meeting is optional. Many teams get by just fine without one.
- It can be less often than daily. Pick the schedule that makes sense to you.
- It should take ~10 minutes, even for large teams.
- This meeting follows a simple formula.

The basic idea is that the team members stand[9] in a circle and answer three questions:

1. What did I do since the last meeting?
2. What will I do until the next meeting?
3. What is in my way?

---

9. This is why it's called a "standup" meeting.

That's all. No discussion. No posturing. No deep explanations. No cold houses nor dark thoughts. No complaints about Jean and Joan and who knows who. Everybody gets 30 seconds or so to answer those three questions. Then the meeting is over and everyone returns to work. Done. Finito. Capisce?

Perhaps the best description of the standup meeting is on Ward's wiki: http://wiki.c2.com/?StandUpMeeting.

PIGS AND CHICKENS?

I won't repeat the ham-and-eggs story here. You can look it up in the footnote[10] if you are interested. The gist is that only developers should speak at the standup. Managers and other folks may listen in but should not interject.

From my point of view, I don't care who speaks so long as everyone follows the same three-question format and the meeting is kept to about 10 minutes.

SHOUT-OUT

One modification that I have enjoyed is to add an optional fourth question:

• Whom do you want to thank?

This is just a quick acknowledgment of someone who helped you or who did something you believe deserves recognition.

CONCLUSION

Agile is a set of principles, practices, and disciplines that help small teams build small software projects. The practices described in this chapter are those that help those small teams behave like true teams. They help the teams set the language they use to communicate, as well as the expectations for how the team members will behave toward each other and toward the project they are building.

---

10. https://en.wikipedia.org/wiki/The_Chicken_and_the_Pig

TECHNICAL PRACTICES

The practices in this chapter describe a radical departure from the way most programmers have behaved during the last 70 years. They enforce a profound minute-by-minute and second-by-second set of ritualistic behaviors that most programmers initially consider absurd. Many programmers have therefore attempted to do Agile without these practices. They fail, however, because these practices are the very core of Agile. Without TDD, Refactoring, Simple Design, and yes, even Pair Programming, Agile becomes an ineffective flaccid shell of what it was intended to be.

TEST-DRIVEN DEVELOPMENT

Test-Driven Development is a rich and complex topic that will require an entire book to cover properly. This chapter is merely an overview that focuses more on justification and motivation than on the deeper technical aspects of the practice. In particular, this chapter will not show any code.

Programmers are engaged in a unique profession. We produce huge documents of deeply technical and arcane symbology. Every symbol written into these documents must be correct; otherwise, truly terrible things can happen. One wrong symbol can result in the loss of fortunes and lives. What other profession is like that?

Accounting. Accountants produce huge documents of deeply technical and arcane symbology. Every symbol written into their documents must be correct lest fortunes, and possibly even lives, be lost. How do accountants ensure that every symbol is correct?

DOUBLE-ENTRY BOOKKEEPING

Accountants have a discipline that was invented 1000 years ago. It's called *double-entry bookkeeping*.[1] Every transaction they enter into their books is entered twice: once as a credit in one set of accounts, and again as a

---

1. https://en.wikipedia.org/wiki/Double-entry_bookkeeping_system

complementary debit in another set of accounts. These accounts eventually flow into a single document called the *balance sheet,* which subtracts the sum of liabilities and equities from the sum of assets. That difference must be zero. If it is not zero, then an error has been made.[2]

Accountants are taught, in the early days of their schooling, to enter the transactions one at a time and compute the balance each time. This allows them to catch errors quickly. They are taught to *avoid* entering a batch of transactions between balance checks, since then errors would be hard to find. This practice is so essential to the proper accounting of monies that it has become *law* in virtually all parts of the world.

Test-Driven Development is the corresponding practice for programmers. Every required behavior is entered twice: once as a test, and then again as production code that makes the test pass. The two entries are complementary, just as assets are complementary to liabilities and equities. When executed together, the two entries produce a zero result: Zero tests failed.

Programmers who learn TDD are taught to enter every behavior one at a time—once as a failing test, and then again as production code that passes the test. This allows them to catch errors quickly. They are taught to avoid writing a lot of production code and then adding a batch of tests, since errors would then be hard to find.

These two disciplines, double-entry bookkeeping and TDD, are equivalent. They both serve the same function: to prevent errors in critically important documents where every symbol must be correct. Despite how essential programming has become to our society, we have not yet imbued TDD with the force of law. But given that lives and fortunes have already been lost to the vagaries of poorly written software, can that law be far away?

---

2. If you have studied accounting, your hair is likely now on fire. Yes, this was a gross simplification. On the other hand, had I described TDD in a single paragraph, all the programmers would set their hair on fire.

THE THREE RULES OF TDD

TDD can be described with three simple rules.

- Do not write any production code until you have first written a test that fails due to the lack of that code.
- Do not write more of a test than is sufficient to fail—and failing to compile counts as a failure.
- Do not write more production code than is sufficient to pass the currently failing test.

A programmer with more than a few months' experience will likely consider these rules to be outlandish, if not downright stupid. They imply a cycle of programming that is perhaps five seconds long. The programmer begins by writing some test code for production code that does not yet exist. This test fails to compile almost immediately because it mentions elements of the production code that have not yet been written. The programmer must stop writing the test and start writing production code. But after only a few keystrokes, the test that failed to compile now compiles properly. This forces the programmer to return to the test and continue to add to it.

This oscillation between the test and the production code is just a few seconds long, and the programmers are trapped within this cycle. The programmers will never again be able to write an entire function, or even a simple `if` statement or `while` loop, without interrupting themselves by writing the complimentary test code.

Most programmers initially view this as a disruption of their thought processes. This continual interruption imposed by the Three Rules prevents them from properly thinking through the code they are writing. They often feel that the Three Rules create an intolerable distraction.

However, imagine a group of programmers following these Three Rules. Choose any one of those programmers you like, at any time. Everything that programmer was working on executed and passed all its tests less than a minute ago. It doesn't matter whom you choose or when you choose them—everything worked less than a minute ago.

DEBUGGING

What would it be like if everything *always* worked a minute ago? How much debugging would you have to do? If everything worked a minute ago, then almost any failure you encounter will be less than a minute old. Debugging a failure that was added in the last minute is often trivial. Indeed, using a debugger to find the problem is probably overkill.

Are you skilled at operating the debugger? Do you have the debugger's hot keys memorized? Does your muscle memory automatically know how to hit those keys to set breakpoints, single-step, step-into, and step-over? When you are debugging, do you feel like you are in your element? *This is not a skill to be desired.*

The only way you get good at using a debugger is by spending a lot of time debugging. Spending a lot of time debugging implies that there are always a lot of bugs. Test-Driven Developers are not skilled at operating the debugger because they simply don't use a debugger that often; and when they do, it is typically for a very brief amount of time.

Now I don't want to create a false impression. Even the best Test-Driven Developer still encounters difficult bugs. This is still software; it's still hard. But the incidence and severity of bugs is vastly reduced by practicing the Three Rules.

DOCUMENTATION

Have you ever integrated a third-party package? It likely came in a zip file that contained some source code, DLLs, JAR files, etc. One of the files in that archive was likely a PDF that contained the instructions for integration. At the end of the PDF, there was probably an ugly appendix with all the code examples.

What was the first thing you read in that document? If you are a programmer, you skipped right to the back and read the code examples because the code will tell you the truth.

When you follow the Three Rules, the tests you end up writing become the code examples for the whole system. If you want to know how to call an API function, there are tests that call that function every way it can be called, catching every exception it can throw. If you want to know how to create an object, there are tests that create that object every way it can be created.

The tests are a form of documentation that describe the system being tested. This documentation is written in a language that the programmers know fluently. It is utterly unambiguous, it is so formal it executes, and it cannot get out of sync with the application code. The tests are the *perfect* kind of documentation for programmers: code.

What's more, the tests do not form a system in and of themselves. The tests don't know about each other. There are no dependencies between the tests. Each test is a small and independent unit of code that describes the way one small part of the system behaves.

Fun

If you have ever written tests after the fact, you know that it's not a lot of fun. It's not fun because you already know the code works. You've tested it manually. You are likely writing those tests because someone told you that you had to. It feels like busy work. It's boring.

When you write the tests first according to the Three Rules, it's fun. Every new test is a challenge. Every time you make a test pass, it's a small success. Your work, as you follow the Three Rules, is a chain of those small challenges and successes. It doesn't feel like busy work—it feels like getting stuff working.

COMPLETENESS

Now let's return to after-the-fact tests. You somehow feel obligated to write these tests even though you've tested the system manually, and you already know it works. You proceed from test to test being unsurprised by the fact that the tests pass.

Inevitably, you will come to a test that's hard to write. It's hard to write because when you wrote the code you weren't thinking about testability, and you did not design it to be testable. To write a test for this code, you are going to have to change the structure by breaking some couplings, adding some abstractions, and/or rerouting some function calls and arguments. This feels like a lot of effort, especially because you already know the code works.

The schedule is tight, and you know you have more pressing things to do. So, you set that test aside. You convince yourself either that it is unnecessary or that you'll go back and write it later. Thus, you leave a hole in the test suite.

And since *you* have left holes in the test suite, you suspect everyone else has, too. When you execute the test suite and see it pass, you laugh, smirk, or derisively wave your hand because you know that the passing of the suite doesn't mean that the system works.

When such a test suite passes, there is no decision you can make. The only information that the passing tests give you is that nothing *tested* is broken. The incompleteness of the test suite leaves you with no options. However, if you follow the Three Rules, then every line of production code was written in order to make a test pass. Therefore, the test suite is very complete. When it passes, you can make a decision. That decision is to *deploy*.

That's the goal. We want to create a suite of automated tests that tells us that it is safe to deploy the system.

Now again, I don't want to paint a false picture. Following the Three Rules will give you a very complete test suite, but it is probably not 100% complete. This is because there are situations in which following the Three Rules is not practical. These situations are outside the scope of this book except to say that they are limited, and there are solutions that mitigate them. The result is that even the most diligent adherents to the Three Rules are not likely to produce a test suite that is 100% complete.

But 100% completeness is not necessary for the deployment decision. Coverage in the high 90s is likely all that is required—and that kind of completeness is eminently achievable.

I have created test suites that are so complete that they allow the deployment decision to be made. I have seen many others do so as well. In each of those cases, the completeness was less than 100%, but it was high enough to make the deployment decision.

Warning

Test coverage is a team metric, not a management metric. Managers are unlikely to know what the metric actually means. *Managers should not use this metric as a goal or a target.* The team should use it solely to inform their testing strategy.

Double Warning

Do not fail the build based on insufficient coverage. If you do this, then the programmers will be forced to remove enough assertions from their tests in order to get the coverage numbers high enough. Code coverage is a complex topic that can only be understood in the context of a deep knowledge of the code and tests. Don't let it become a management metric.

DESIGN

Remember that function that's hard to test after the fact? It may be hard to test because it is coupled to behaviors that you'd rather not execute in the test. For example, it might turn on the x-ray machine or delete rows out of the database. The function is hard to test because you did not design it to be easy to test. You wrote the code first, and you are now writing the tests as an afterthought. Designing for testability was the furthest thing from your mind when you wrote the code.

Now you are faced with redesigning the code in order to test it. You look at your watch and realize that this whole testing thing has taken too long already. Since you've already tested it manually, and you know it works, you walk away, leaving yet another hole in the test suite.

However, when you write the test first, something very different happens. You *cannot* write a function that is hard to test. Since you are writing the test first, you will naturally design the function you are testing to be easy to test. How do you keep functions easy to test? You decouple them. Indeed, testability is just a synonym for decoupling.

By writing the tests first, you will decouple the system in ways that you had never thought about before. The whole system will be testable; therefore, the whole system will be decoupled.

It is for this reason that TDD is often called a design technique. The Three Rules force you into a much higher degree of decoupling.

COURAGE

So far, we've seen that following the Three Rules provides a number of powerful benefits: less debugging, good low-level documentation, fun, completeness, and decoupling. But these are just ancillary benefits; none of these is the driving reason for practicing TDD. The real reason is courage.

I told you the following story at the beginning of the book, but it bears repeating here.

Imagine that you are looking at some old code on your screen, and it's a mess. You think to yourself, "I should clean this up." But your next thought is, "I'm not touching it!" Because you know if you touch it, you will break it; and if you break it, it becomes yours. So you back away from the code, leaving the mess to fester and rot.

This is a fear reaction. You fear the code. You fear touching it. You fear what will happen to you if you break it. So, you fail to do the one thing that could improve the code—you fail to clean it.

If everyone on the team behaves this way, then the code must rot. No one will clean it. No one will improve it. Every feature added will be added in such a way as to minimize the immediate risk to the programmers. Couplings and duplications will be added because they minimize the immediate risk, even though they corrupt the design and integrity of the code.

Eventually the code will become such a horrible mass of unmaintainable spaghetti that little to no progress can be made with it. Estimates will grow exponentially. Managers will become desperate. More and more programmers will be hired in the hopes of increasing productivity, but that increase will not be realized.

Finally, in utter desperation, the managers will agree to the programmers' demands that the whole system should be rewritten from scratch, and the cycle will begin again.

Imagine a different scenario. Go back to that screen with the messy code. Your first thought was to clean it. What if you had a test suite that was so complete that you trusted it when it passed? What if that test suite ran quickly? What would your next thought be? It would be something like this:

> *Gosh, I think I'll change the name of that variable. Ah, the tests still pass. OK, now I'll split that big function into two smaller functions... Good, the tests still pass.... OK, now I think I can move one of those new functions over into a different class. Whoops! The tests failed. Put it back... Ah, I see, I needed to move that variable as well. Yes, the tests still pass...*

When you have a complete test suite, you lose your fear of changing the code. You lose your fear of *cleaning* the code. So, you *will* clean the code. You will keep the system neat and orderly. You will keep the design of the system intact. You will *not* create the festering mass of spaghetti that would drag the team into the doldrums of low productivity and eventual failure.

That is why we practice TDD. We practice it because it gives us the courage to keep the code clean and orderly. It gives us the courage to act like professionals.

REFACTORING

Refactoring is another one of those topics that requires a book to describe. Fortunately, Martin Fowler has done a superb job with just such a book.[3] In this chapter I'll simply discuss the discipline, not the specific techniques. Again, this chapter contains no code.

Refactoring is the practice of *improving* the structure of the code without altering the behavior, as defined by the tests. In other words, we make changes to the names, the classes, the functions, and the expressions without breaking any of the tests. We improve the structure of the system, without affecting the behavior.

Of course, this practice couples strongly with TDD. To fearlessly refactor the code, we need a test suite that gives us very high confidence that we aren't breaking anything.

The kinds of changes made during refactoring range from trivial cosmetics to deep restructurings. The changes might be simple name changes or complex reshufflings of switch statements to polymorphic dispatches. Large functions will be split into smaller, better-named, functions. Argument lists will be changed into objects. Classes with many methods will be split into many

---

3. Fowler, M. 2019. *Refactoring: Improving the Design of Existing Code*, 2nd ed. Boston, MA: Addison-Wesley.

smaller classes. Functions will be moved from one class to another. Classes will be extracted into subclasses or inner classes. Dependencies will be inverted, and modules will be moved across architectural boundaries.

And while all this is taking place, we keep the tests continuously passing.

RED/GREEN/REFACTOR

The process of refactoring is woven intrinsically into the Three Rules of TDD in what is known as the Red/Green/Refactor cycle (Figure 5.1).

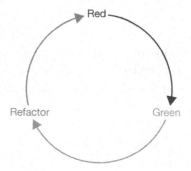

Figure 5.1 The Red/Green/Refactor cycle

1. First, we create a test that fails.
2. Then we make the test pass.
3. Then we clean up the code.
4. Return to step 1.

The idea here is that writing code that *works* and writing code that is *clean* are two separate dimensions of programming. Attempting to control both dimensions at the same time is difficult at best, so we separate the two dimensions into two different activities.

To say this differently, it is hard enough to get code working, let alone getting the code to be clean. So we first focus on getting the code working by whatever messy means occur to our meager minds. Then, once working, with tests passing, we clean up the mess we made.

This makes it clear that refactoring is a *continuous* process, and not one that is performed on a scheduled basis. We don't make a huge mess for days and days, and then try to clean it up. Rather, we make a very small mess, over a period of a minute or two, and then we clean up that small mess.

The word *Refactoring* should never appear on a schedule. Refactoring is not the kind of activity that appears on a plan. We do not reserve time for refactoring. Refactoring is simply part of our minute-by-minute, hour-by-hour approach to writing software.

BIGGER REFACTORINGS

Sometimes the requirements change in such a way that you realize the current design and architecture of the system is suboptimal, and you need to make a significant change to the structure of the system. Such changes are made *within* the Red/Green/Refactor cycle. We do not create a project specifically to change the design. We do not reserve time in the schedule for such large refactorings. Instead, we migrate the code one small step at a time, while continuing to add new features during the normal Agile cycle.

Such a change to the design may take place over several days, weeks, or even months. During that time, the system continues to pass all its tests and may be deployed to production, even though the design transition is only partially complete.

SIMPLE DESIGN

The practice of Simple Design is one of the goals of Refactoring. Simple Design is the practice of writing only the code that is required with a structure that keeps it simplest, smallest, and most expressive.

Kent Beck's rules of Simple Design are as follows:

1. Pass all the tests.
2. Reveal the intent.

3. Remove duplication.

4. Decrease elements.

The numbers are both the order in which these are executed and the priority they are given.

Point 1 is self-evident. The code must pass all the tests. The code must work.

Point 2 says that after the code is made to work, it should then be made expressive. It should reveal the intention of the programmer. It should be easy to read and self-descriptive. This is where we apply many of the simpler and more cosmetic refactorings. We also split large functions into smaller, better-named functions.

Point 3 says that after we have made the code as descriptive and expressive as possible, we hunt for and remove any duplication within that code. We don't want the code to say the same thing more than once. During this activity, the refactorings are usually more complicated. Sometimes removing duplication is as simple as moving the duplicate code into a function and calling it from many places. Other times it requires more interesting solutions, such as the Design Patterns:[4] *Template Method, Strategy, Decorator,* or *Visitor.*

Point 4 says that once we have removed all the duplication, we should strive to decrease the number of structural elements, such as classes, functions, variables, etc.

The goal of Simple Design is to keep the *design weight* of the code as small as practicable.

---

4. Design Patterns are beyond the scope of this book. See Gamma, E., R. Helm, R. Johnson, and J. Vlissides. 1995. *Design Patterns: Elements of Reusable Object-Oriented Software.* Reading, MA: Addison-Wesley.

DESIGN WEIGHT

The designs of a software system range from quite simple to extraordinarily complex. The more complex the design, the greater the cognitive load placed on the programmers. That cognitive load is *Design Weight*. The greater the weight of that design, the more time and effort are required for the programmers to understand and manipulate the system.

Similarly, the complexity of the requirements also ranges from very small to very great. The greater the complexity of the requirements, the more time and effort are required to understand and manipulate the system.

However, the two factors are not additive. Complex requirements can be *simplified* by employing a more complex design. Often the trade-off is favorable. The overall complexity of the system can be reduced by choosing the appropriate design for an existing set of features.

Achieving this balance of design and feature complexity is the goal of Simple Design. Using this practice, programmers continuously refactor the design of the system to keep it in balance with the requirements and, therefore, keep productivity maximized.

PAIR PROGRAMMING

The practice of *Pair Programming* has enjoyed a substantial amount of controversy and disinformation over the years. Many folks react negatively to the idea that two (or more) people can work productively together on the same problem.

First of all, pairing is optional. No one should be forced to pair. Secondly, pairing is intermittent. There are many good reasons to code alone from time to time. The amount of pairing a team should engage in is 50% or so. That number is not critical. It could be as low as 30% or as much as 80%. For the most part, this is an individual and team choice.

WHAT IS PAIRING?

Pairing is the act of two people working together on a single programming problem. The pair may work together at the same workstation, sharing the screen, keyboard, and mouse. Or they may work on two connected workstations so long as they see and manipulate the same code. The latter option works nicely with popular screen-sharing software. That software also allows the partners to be remote from each other, so long as they have a good data and voice link.

Pairing programmers sometimes adopt different roles. One may be the driver and the other the navigator. The driver has the keyboard and mouse; the navigator takes a longer view and makes recommendations. Another role option is for one programmer to write a test, and the other to make it pass and write the next test for the first programmer to pass. This is sometimes called *Ping-Pong*.

Most often, however, there are no roles at all. The programmers are simply co-equal authors sharing the mouse and keyboard in a cooperative manner.

Pairs are not scheduled. They form and break up according to the programmers' preference. Managers should not try to create pairing schedules or pairing matrices.

Pairs are generally short-lived. A pairing session can last as long as a day, but more often they last no more than an hour or two. Even pairings as short as 15 to 30 minutes can be beneficial.

Stories are not assigned to pairs. Individual programmers, and not pairs, are responsible for completing stories. The duration of a story is generally much longer than a single pairing.

Over the course of a week, each programmer will spend about half of their pairing time on their own tasks, recruiting the help of several others. The other half of their pairing time will be spent helping others with their tasks.

Seniors should take care to pair with juniors more often than they pair with other seniors. Juniors should request the help of seniors more often than they request the help of other juniors. Programmers with specialties should spend significant amounts of their pairing time working with programmers outside of their specialty. The goal is to spread and exchange knowledge, not concentrate it.

Why Pair?

We pair so that we behave like a team. The members of a team do not work in isolation from each other. Instead, they collaborate on a second-by-second basis. When a member of a team goes down, the other team members cover the hole left by that member and keep making progress towards the goal.

Pairing is the best way, by far, to share knowledge between team members and prevent knowledge silos from forming. It is the best way to make sure that nobody on the team is indispensable.

Many teams have reported that pairing reduces errors and improves design quality. This is likely true in most cases. It is generally better to have more than one set of eyes on any given problem. Indeed, many teams have replaced code reviews with pairing.

Pairing as Code Review

Pairing is a form of code review, but with a significant advantage. The pairing programmers are co-authors during the time they are pairing. They see older code and review it as a matter of course, but with the intention of authoring new code. Thus, the review is not simply a static check to ensure that the team's coding standards are applied. Rather, it is a dynamic review of the current state of the code with an eye to where the code needs to be in the near future.

WHAT ABOUT THE COST?

It is hard to measure the cost of pairing. The most direct cost is that there are two people working on a single problem. It should be obvious that this does not double the effort to solve the problem; however, it does likely cost something. Various studies have indicated that the direct cost might be about 15%. In other words, it would require 115 pairing programmers to do the same work of 100 individuals (without code reviews).

A naive calculation would suggest that a team that pairs 50% of the time would suffer something less than 8% in productivity. On the other hand, if the practice of pairing replaces code reviews, then there is likely no reduction in productivity at all.

Then we must consider the benefits of the cross-training knowledge exchange and intense collaboration. These benefits are not easily quantifiable, but they are also likely significant.

My experience and the experience of many others is that pairing, when done informally and at the programmers' discretion, is quite beneficial to the whole team.

JUST TWO?

The word "pair" implies that there are just two programmers involved in a pairing session. While this is typically true, it is not a rule. Sometimes three, four, or more will decide to work together on a given problem. (Again, this is at the programmers' discretion.) This is sometimes known as "mob programming."[5,6]

MANAGEMENT

Programmers often fear that managers will frown upon pairing and might even demand that pairs break up and stop wasting time. I've never seen this

---

5. https://en.wikipedia.org/wiki/Mob_programming
6. https://mobprogramming.org/mob-programming-basics/

happen. In the half-century that I've been writing code, I've never seen a manager interfere at such a low level. Generally, in my experience, managers are pleased to see programmers collaborating and working together. It creates the impression that work is being done.

If, however, you are a manager who is tempted to interfere with pairing because you fear it is inefficient, then set your fears aside and let the programmers figure this out. They are, after all, the experts. And if you are a programmer whose manager has told you to stop pairing, remind that manager that you are the expert, and that therefore you, and not the manager, must be in charge of the way you work.

Finally, never, ever, ever, ask for permission to pair. Or test. Or refactor. Or... You are the expert. You decide.

CONCLUSION

The technical practices of Agile are the most essential ingredient of any Agile effort. Any attempt to employ Agile practices without the technical practices is doomed to fail. The reason for this is simply that Agile is an efficient mechanism for making a big mess in a big hurry. Without the technical practices to keep the technical quality high, the productivity of the team will quickly falter and begin an inexorable death spiral.

BECOMING 6 AGILE

When I first learned about XP, I thought, "What could be easier? Just follow a few simple disciplines and practices. Nothing to it."

However, based upon the number of organizations that try—and fail—to become Agile, becoming Agile must be very, very difficult. Perhaps the reason for all that failure is that so many organizations think Agile is something that it's not.

AGILE VALUES

Kent Beck named the four values of Agile long ago. They are courage, communication, feedback, and simplicity.

COURAGE

The first value is courage—or, in other words, a reasonable degree of risk-taking. The members of an Agile team are not so focused upon political safety that they sacrifice quality and opportunity. They realize that the best way to manage a software project over the long term is with a certain degree of aggression.

There is a difference between courage and recklessness. It requires courage to deploy a minimum feature set. It also requires courage to maintain high code quality and maintain high-quality disciplines. However, it is reckless to deploy code that you are not highly confident in or that has an unsustainable design. It is reckless to conform to a schedule by sacrificing quality.

The belief that quality and discipline *increase* speed is a courageous belief because it will constantly be challenged by powerful but naive folks who are in a hurry.

COMMUNICATION

We value direct and frequent communication that crosses channels. Agile team members want to talk with one another. The programmers, customers, testers, and managers want to sit near each other and interact with each other frequently, and not just in the context of meetings. Not just through emails, chat, and memos. Rather, they value face-to-face, informal, interpersonal conversation.

This is how teams gel. It is within the rapid, chaotic, informal firestorm of frequent interaction that light bulbs go off and insight is gained. A team that sits together and communicates frequently can work miracles.

FEEDBACK

The Agile disciplines we have studied are virtually all geared toward providing rapid feedback to the folks who make important decisions. *Planning Game, Refactoring, Test Driven Development, Continuous Integration, Small Releases, Collective Ownership, Whole Team,* etc. *maximize* the frequency and quantity of feedback. They allow us to determine when things are going wrong early enough to correct them. They provide massive education about the consequences of earlier decisions. Agile teams *thrive* on feedback. Feedback is what makes the team work so effectively and what drives a project to a beneficial outcome.

SIMPLICITY

The next Agile value is simplicity—in other words, *being direct*. It has often been said that every problem in software can be solved by adding another layer of indirection. But the values of courage, communication, and feedback are there to ensure that the number of problems is reduced to a minimum. Therefore, indirection can be kept to a minimum. Solutions can be simple.

This applies to the software, but it also applies to the team. Passive aggression is indirection. When you recognize a problem but silently allow it to pass to someone else, you are engaging in indirection. When you accede to the demands of a manager or customer knowing that the consequences will be dire, you are being indirect.

Simplicity is directness—directness in the code, and directness in communication and behavior. In the code, a certain amount of indirection is necessary. Indirection is the mechanism by which we reduce the complexity of interdependence. On the team, far less indirection is necessary. Most of the time, you want to be as direct as possible.

Keep the code simple. Keep the team simpler.

THE MENAGERIE

It is easy to become confused by the vast numbers of Agile methods out there. My advice to you is to ignore the menagerie. In the end, regardless of which method you choose, you will wind up tuning and tweaking the process to fit your own needs. Thus, whether you begin with XP, Scrum, or any of the 5328 other Agile methods out there, you are going to wind up in the same place.

The strongest advice I can give you, however, is to adopt the full Circle of Life, including, and most especially, the technical practices. Far too many teams have adopted the outer business ring and have found themselves in the trap that Martin Fowler has labeled "Flaccid Scrum."[1] The symptoms of this disease are a slow decline from high productivity in the early days of a project to very low productivity as the project wears on. The reason for this loss of productivity is the corruption and degradation of the code itself.

It turns out that the business practices of Agile are a highly efficient way to make a very large mess. Furthermore, if you don't take care of the cleanliness of the structure you are building, then the mess will slow you *way* down.

So, pick one of the methods or none of the methods. Ensure that you address all the disciplines in the Circle of Life. Get the team to agree. Then, begin. Remember courage, communication, feedback, and simplicity and regularly adjust the disciplines and behaviors. Don't ask for permission. Don't stress about "doing it right." Just work through the issues as they arise and continue to drive your projects to the best possible outcome.

---

1. https://martinfowler.com/bliki/FlaccidScrum.html

TRANSFORMATION

The transition from non-Agile to Agile is a transition in values. The values of Agile development include risk-taking, rapid-feedback, intense, high-bandwidth communication between people that ignores barriers and command structures. They also focus on moving in straight and direct lines rather than mapping out and negotiating the landscape. These values are diametrically opposed to the values of large organizations who have invested heavily in middle-management structures that value safety, consistency, command-and-control, and plan execution.

Is it possible to transform such an organization to Agile? Frankly, this is not something I have had a lot of success with, nor have I seen much success from others. I have seen plenty of effort and money expended, but I have not seen many organizations that truly make the transition. The value structures are just too different for the middle-management layer to accept.

What I *have* seen is the transition of teams and individuals, because teams and individuals are often directed by values that are aligned with Agile.

Ironically, executives are also often driven by the risk-taking, direct, communicative values of Agile. This is one of the reasons they try to transition their organizations.

The barrier is the management layer in the middle. These folks were hired to *not* take risks, to *avoid* directness, to *follow* and *enforce* the chain of command with a *minimum* of communication. This is the organizational dilemma. The tops and bottoms of the organization value the Agile mindset, but the middle layer opposes it. I don't know that I have ever seen that middle layer make the change. Indeed, how could they? Their job is to *oppose* such a change.

To drive this point home, let me tell you a few stories.

THE SUBTERFUGE

In one Agile transformation in which I participated back in 2000, we had the support of the executives and the programmers. There was a lot of hopeful enthusiasm. The problem was the technical leads and architects. These folks incorrectly surmised that their roles were being diminished.

The roles of architects, technical leads, project managers, and many others are different in an Agile team, but they are not diminished. Unfortunately, these folks could not see this, and that may have been our fault. Perhaps we did not communicate how valuable their roles were to the team, or perhaps they were just uncomfortable learning the new skills they'd need.

In any event, they met in secret and devised plans to sabotage the Agile transition. I won't go into the details of that plan. I'll just say that they were caught at it, and they were immediately fired.

I'd like to report that the Agile Transition then proceeded apace and achieved great success. But I can't.

THE LION CUBS

We had great success transitioning one division of a much larger company. They adopted XP and did such great work over the years that they were written up in *Computerworld*. In fact, all that success led to the promotion of the VP of engineering who led that transition.

Then the new VP took over. And like a new male lion taking over the pride, he proceeded to kill all the offspring of the previous VP. And that included Agile. He stopped it cold and reverted the team to their old, far less successful process.

This led many folks on the team to seek employment elsewhere—which, I believe, was the new VP's intent.

WEEPING

This last story is second hand. I wasn't there to witness the critical moment. It was reported to me by my employees at the time.

In 2003, my company participated in an Agile Transition at a well-known stock brokerage firm. All was proceeding well. We trained the executives, the middle managers, and the developers. They were cooking along. Everything was going great.

Then came the final assessment. The executives, middle managers, and developers all met in a big auditorium. Their goal was to assess the progress and success of the Agile Transition. The executives asked the question, "How's it going?"

The answer came from the various participants: "It's going very well."

Then there was a moment of silence in the room, which was suddenly punctuated by the sound of someone in the back of the room, weeping. And that's when the emotional supports crumbled, and the positive mood in the room collapsed. "This is just too hard." People were heard to say. "We just can't keep this up."

And so, the executives killed the transition.

MORAL

I suppose the moral of all these stories is "Expect something weird to happen."

FAKING IT

Can Agile teams exist in an organization with a strong middle-management layer that opposes Agile? I have seen this happen upon occasion. Some software development teams quietly use Agile values to drive their development, while also conforming to the rigors imposed upon them by middle management. So long as middle management is satisfied that their procedures and standards are being followed, they may leave the development teams to their own devices.

This is what Booch and Parnas called "faking it."[2] The team does Agile under the covers, while providing everything that satisfies the middle-management layer. Rather than fighting a futile battle with the middle managers, these teams put a layer on top of Agile that makes Agile look safe and conformant to the middle managers.

For example, the middle managers may want an analysis document produced in the early phases of the project. The Agile team provides this document by writing much of the early code of the system using all the normal Agile disciplines, and then produces the analysis document by scheduling a sequence of documentation stories.

This makes sense because the first few coding iterations are heavily focused on requirements analysis. The fact that this analysis is being done by actually writing code is not something that the middle managers need to know. Nor should they care.

Unfortunately, I have seen organizations who are so dysfunctional that when middle managers smell that a team is "faking it," they assume subterfuge and quickly move to expunge the Agile disciplines. This is a deep shame because those teams were actually giving the middle managers what they needed.

SUCCESS IN SMALLER ORGANIZATIONS

I have seen some medium-sized organizations adopt Agile. They had thin middle-management layers composed of folks who came up through the ranks and still retained the direct, risk-taking mindset.

---

2. Booch, G. 1994. *Object-Oriented Analysis and Design with Applications*, 2nd ed. Reading, MA: Addison-Wesley, p. 233–34.

It is not uncommon to see small organizations transition completely to Agile. They have no middle management, and the values of the executives and developers are strongly aligned.

INDIVIDUAL SUCCESS AND MIGRATION

Finally, sometimes only certain individuals within an organization adopt the Agile values. Individuals who make this transition do not fare well within organizations or teams who do not. The difference in values generally leads to a separation of some kind. In the best case, the individuals who make the transition will join to form new Agile teams that manage to hide from middle management. If that's not possible, they will likely seek (and find) employment at a company that shares their values.

Indeed, over the last twenty years, we have seen this migration of values taking place in the industry. New companies that embrace the Agile values have been formed, and programmers who desire to work in an Agile manner flock to those companies.

CREATING AGILE ORGANIZATIONS

Can large organizations be created that allow Agile teams to prosper within them? Certainly! However, note that the word is *created* not *transformed*.

When IBM decided to build the PC, the company's executives realized that the values of the organization would not allow the kind of quick innovation and risk-taking that would be required. So, they *created* an organization with a different value structure.[3]

Have we seen this happen in the software world? Have older, large organizations *created* smaller software organizations for the purpose of adopting Agile? I've seen hints of this, but I cannot bring to mind any overt examples. We have certainly seen many startups adopt Agile. We have also seen many Agile consulting companies being used by large non-Agile

---

3. The birth of the IBM PC. Accessed at https://www.ibm.com/ibm/history/exhibits/pc25/pc25_birth.html.

companies that want to get certain software projects done more quickly and reliably.

That's my prediction. We will eventually see larger companies create new divisions that use Agile for their software development. We will also see Agile consulting companies used more and more by larger organizations that have been unable to transform their existing development staff.

COACHING

Does an Agile team need a coach? The short answer is "No." The longer answer is "Sometimes."

First, we need to differentiate between Agile trainers and Agile coaches. An Agile trainer teaches a team how to conduct themselves in an Agile way. They are often hired from outside the company or are internal trainers from outside the team. Their goal is to inculcate the Agile values and teach the Agile disciplines. Their tenure should be short. Each team of a dozen or so developers should require no more than one or two weeks of training. Everything else they need to learn they're going to learn by themselves no matter what the Agile trainer says or does.

Early in the transition of a team, a trainer may temporarily fill the role of the coach, but this is a temporary situation. That role should be filled from within the team as soon as possible.

In general, Agile coaches are not trainers. They are members of the team whose role is to defend the process within the team. In the heat of development, developers may be tempted to go off process. Perhaps they inadvertently stop pairing, stop refactoring, or ignore failures in the continuous build. It is the coach's job to see this and point it out to the team. The coach acts as the team's conscience, always reminding the team of the promises they made to themselves and the values they agreed to hold.

This role typically rotates from one team member to the next on an informal schedule and based on need. A mature team working steadily along does not require a coach. On the other hand, a team under some kind of stress—whether it be schedule, business, or interpersonal—may decide to ask someone to fill the role temporarily.

The coach is not a manager. The coach is not responsible for budget or schedule. The coach does not direct the team nor does she represent the team's interests to management. The coach is not the liaison between the customers and the developers. The role of the coach is strictly internal to the team. Neither the managers nor the customers know who the coach is, nor even whether there currently is a coach.

Scrum Masters

In Scrum, the coach is called a *Scrum Master*. The invention of this term, and the sequence of events that followed it, were among the best and worst things that happened to the Agile community. The certification programs attracted large numbers of project managers. This influx increased the popularity of Agile in the early days but eventually led to the role of the coach to be conflated with the role of the project manager.

Nowadays, it is all too frequent that we see Scrum Masters who are not coaches at all but are simply project managers doing what project managers always did. Unfortunately, the title and certification tend to give them undue influence over the Agile team.

Certification

The Agile certifications that exist are a complete joke and an utter absurdity. Do not take the certifications seriously. The training that accompanies the certification programs is often worthwhile; however, that training should not be focused on a particular role, it should be for everyone on the team.

For example, the fact that someone is "certified" a Scrum Master is a worthless certification. The certifiers are not guaranteeing anything other than that the person paid the fee for, and possibly attended, a two-day course. The certifiers are specifically *not* guaranteeing that the newly minted Scrum Master will do a good job as a coach. The absurd implication of the certification is that there is something special about a "Certified Scrum Master," which of course flies in the face of the notion of a coach. An Agile coach is not specially trained to be an Agile coach.

Again, there's often nothing wrong with the training programs that go along with these certifications. However, it is foolish to train just one special person. Every member of an Agile team needs to understand the values and techniques of Agile. Therefore, if one member of the team is trained, all members of the team should be trained.

REAL CERTIFICATION

What would a real Agile certification program look like? It would be a semester-long course, complete with Agile training and the supervised development of a small Agile project. The course would be graded and the students held to a high bar. The certifier would guarantee that the students understood Agile values and showed proficiency in executing Agile disciplines.

AGILE IN THE LARGE

The Agile movement began in the late '80s. It was quickly recognized as a means for organizing a small team of between 4 and 12 software developers. Those numbers are soft and were seldom articulated, but everyone understood that Agile (or whatever we called it before 2001) was not appropriate for a massive team of thousands of developers. That was not the problem we were trying to solve.

Nevertheless, almost immediately, the question was raised. What about big teams? What about Agile in the large?

Over the years, many folks have tried to answer that question. Early on, the authors of Scrum proposed the so-called "Scrum-of-Scrums" technique. Later, we started to see certain branded approaches like SAFe[4] and LeSS.[5] Several books have since been written on the topic.

I'm sure there's nothing wrong with these approaches. I'm sure the books are fine. But I haven't tried the approaches, and I haven't read the books. You might think that it is irresponsible of me to comment on a topic that I have not studied. You may be right. However, I have a certain perspective.

Agile is for small- to medium-sized teams, period. It works well for such teams. Agile was never intended for large teams.

Why weren't we trying to solve the problem of large teams? Simply because the problem of large teams is a problem that many experts have worked on for well over five millennia. The problem of large teams is the problem of societies and civilizations. And, if our current civilization is any measure, it appears to be a problem that we have solved rather well.

How do you build the pyramids? You need to have solved the problem of large teams. How do you win World War II? You need to have solved the problem of large teams. How do you send men to the moon and bring them safely back to Earth? You need to have solved the problem of large teams.

But those big projects aren't the only large-team accomplishments we see, are they? How do you build the telephone network, or the highway network, or the internet, or iPhones, or automobiles? All of this is about large teams. The infrastructure and defense of our vast, globe-spanning, civilization is proof that we have solved the problem of large teams.

Large teams are a solved problem.

---

4. https://en.wikipedia.org/wiki/Scaled_agile_framework
5. https://less.works/

The problem that was not solved back in the late '80s when the Agile movement began was the problem of *small software* teams. We did not know how to effectively organize a relatively small group of programmers to be effective. And it was *this* problem that Agile solved.

It's important to understand that this was a *software* problem, not a small team problem. The problem of small teams had been solved millennia before by military and industrial organizations around the world. The Romans could not have conquered Europe if they had not solved the problem of organizing small squads.

Agile is the set of disciplines by which we organize small software teams. Why do we need a special technique for this? Because software is unique. There are very few tasks like it. The cost/benefit and risk/reward trade-offs in software are different from just about every other kind of work. Software is like building, except nothing physical gets built. Software is like mathematics, except that nothing can be proven. Software is as empirical as science, but there are no physical laws to be discovered. Software is like accounting, except it describes time-ordered behavior instead of numerical facts.

Software is really like nothing else. So in order to organize a small team of software developers, we need a special set of disciplines that are tuned to the unique aspects of software.

Look back through the disciplines and practices that we've been talking about in this book. You'll note that each one of them, almost without exception, is tweaked and tuned specifically for the unique aspects of software. This ranges from the obvious practices like Test Driven Development and Refactoring to the more subtle implications of The Planning Game.

The bottom line here is that *Agile is about software*. In particular, it is about *small software teams*. I am always frustrated when people ask me how to apply Agile to hardware, construction, or some other task. My answer has always been that I don't know, because Agile is about software.

What about Agile in the large? *I don't think there is such a thing.* Organizing large teams is a matter of organizing them into small teams. Agile solves the problem for small software teams; the problem of organizing small teams into larger teams is a solved problem. Therefore, my answer to the question of Agile in the large is simply to organize your developers into small Agile teams, then use standard management and operations research techniques to manage those teams. You don't need any other special rules.

Now the question that could be asked is that, since software for small teams was so unique that it required us to invent Agile, why doesn't that uniqueness hold for organizing small software teams into larger software teams? Isn't there some unique aspect to software that carries beyond the small team and affects the way larger teams ought to be organized?

I doubt it, because the problem of large teams, which we solved more than 5000 years ago, *is* the problem of getting many diverse kinds of teams to cooperate. Agile teams are just one of myriad kinds of teams that need to be coordinated in a large project. The integration of diverse teams is a solved problem. I see no indication that the uniqueness of software teams unduly affects their integration into larger teams.

So again, the bottom line from my point of view is this: There is no such thing as Agile in the large. Agile was a necessary innovation for organizing small software teams. But once organized, those teams fit into the structure that large organizations have used for millennia.

Now, again, this is not a subject that I have diligently researched. What you just read is my opinion, and I could be very wrong. Perhaps I'm the old curmudgeon telling all those Agile-in-the-large kids to get off my lawn. Time will tell. But now you know which way I'm betting.

AGILE TOOLS

By Tim Ottinger and Jeff Langr, April 16, 2019[*]

Makers master their tools. Carpenters become adept with hammer, measure, saw, chisel, plane, and level—all inexpensive tools—during the first steps of their career. As their needs grow, carpenters learn and employ more powerful tools (which are usually more expensive): drill, nail gun, lathe, router, CAD, and CNC to name a few.

However, master carpenters don't abandon hand tools; they choose the right tool for the job. Using only hand tools, skilled makers can craft wood projects with higher quality and sometimes faster than with power tools. As a result, wise carpenters master their hand tools before moving on to tools that are more sophisticated. They learn the limits of the hand tools so that they know when to reach for a power tool.

Regardless of whether they use hand or power tools, carpenters always seek to master each implement they choose for their toolbox. This mastery allows them to focus on the craft itself—the delicate shaping of a high-quality piece of furniture, for example—rather than the tool. Without mastery, a tool becomes an impediment to delivery, and a poorly used tool can even cause harm to the project and its operator.

SOFTWARE TOOLS

Software developers must master a number of core tools:

- At least one programming language, and often more
- An integrated development environment or programmer's editor (vim, Emacs, etc.)
- Various data formats (JSON, XML, YAML, etc.) and markup languages (including HTML)
- Command-line and script-based interaction with the operating system
- Source repository tools (Git. Is there another choice?)

---

[*] Used with permission.

- Continuous integration/build tools (Jenkins, TeamCity, GoCD, etc.)
- Deployment/server management tools (Docker, Kubernetes, Ansible, Chef, Puppet, etc.)
- Communication tools: email, Slack, the English language (!)
- Testing tools (unit testing frameworks, Cucumber, Selenium, etc.)

These categories of tools are essential to building software. Without them, it is impossible to deliver anything in today's world. In a sense, they represent the programmer's toolbox of "hand tools."

Many of these tools demand hard-earned expertise for effective use. The landscape meanwhile changes constantly, making tool mastery even more challenging. The savvy developer finds the path of least resistance and highest value through all the tools involved: what gives the biggest bang for the buck?

WHAT MAKES FOR AN EFFECTIVE TOOL?

The tool landscape changes rapidly because we are always learning more effective ways to accomplish our goals. Witness the wide variety of source repository tools introduced in the past few decades: PVCS, ClearCase, Microsoft Visual SourceSafe, StarTeam, Perforce, CVS, Subversion, and Mercurial, to name a few. All suffered problems—too flaky, too proprietary or closed, too slow, too invasive, too scary, too complex. A winner eventually emerged, one that managed to overcome most objections: Git.

One of the most empowering aspects of Git is its ability to make you feel safe. If you were around long enough to have used one of the other tools, you likely felt a little nervous from time to time. You needed a live network connection to the server, or your work was at risk. The CVS repository would get corrupted occasionally, requiring you to muck around in its attic to hopefully uncorrupt things. The repository server crashed sometimes; even if it was backed up, you risked losing half a day's work. Some proprietary tools suffered repository corruption, meaning you'd be on the phone for hours with support while soliciting donations for the king's ransom needed to pay for uncorrupting it. With Subversion, you'd fear doing much branching because the more source files that were involved, the longer you'd have to wait when switching branches (we're talking many minutes here).

A good tool should feel comfortable in your hands and not make you queasy with the dread of having to use it. Git is quick, it gives you the ability to commit locally instead of only to a server, it allows you to work from your local repository without a network connection, it handles multiple repositories and multiple branches well, and it deftly supports merges.

The interface to Git is fairly streamlined and direct. As a result, once you've learned Git well enough, you don't think much about the tool itself. You instead focus on the real needs: safe storage, integration, and management of source code versions. The tool has become *transparent*.

Git is a powerful and complex tool, so just what does it mean to learn it "well enough"? Fortunately, the 80/20 rule applies: a small fraction of Git's capabilities—20%, perhaps—gets you well over 80% of the day-to-day needs you'll have for source management. You can learn most of what you need in minutes. The rest is available online.

The simplicity and effectiveness of using Git led to wholly unplanned, new ways of thinking about how to build software. Linus Torvalds probably would have thought it was insane to use Git as a tool to quickly throw away bits of code, but that's exactly what proponents of the Mikado Method[6] and TCR (Test && Commit || Revert)[7] promote. And even though a key, powerful aspect of Git is its ability to handle branches very effectively, countless teams almost exclusively do trunk-based development while using Git. The tool is *exapted* (used effectively in ways the originators hadn't intended).

Great tools do the following:

- Help people accomplish their objectives
- Can be learned "well enough" quickly

---

6. Ellnestam, O., and D. Broland. 2014. *The Mikado Method*. Shelter Island, NY: Manning Publications.
7. Beck, K. 2018. *test && commit || revert*. Accessed at https://medium.com/@kentbeck_7670/test-commit-revert-870bbd756864.

- Become transparent to users
- Allow adaptation and exaptation
- Are affordable

We hold up Git here as an example of a great tool…as of 2019. You may be reading this in some future year, so remember that the landscape changes.

PHYSICAL AGILE TOOLS

Agilists are known for using whiteboards, tape, index cards, markers, and various sizes of sticky notes (small and flip-chart-size) for visual management of their work. These simple "hand implements" have all the qualities of a great tool:

- They help make work in progress visible and manageable.
- They're intuitive—no training required!
- They require negligible cognitive overhead. You can use them easily while concentrating on other tasks.
- They're easily exapted. None of these tools was designed expressly for managing software development.
- They're adaptable. You can use tape or sticky putty with them, clip pictures or icons to them, tape additional indicators to them, and add nuance of meaning through novel use of custom colors and iconography.
- They're all inexpensive and easily acquired.

Co-located teams can easily manage huge and complex projects using only these simple and inexpensive physical tools. You can radiate key information using a flip chart sheet taped to a wall. Such *information radiators* summarize important trends and facts for team members and sponsors alike. You can use these information radiators to devise and present new kinds of information on the fly. The flexibility is nearly infinite.

Every tool has its limitations. One key limitation of physical tools is that they're not very effective for distributed teams, only for people within visual range. The physical tools also don't automatically maintain history—you have only the current state.

THE PRESSURE TO AUTOMATE

The original XP project (C3) was largely managed with physical tools. As Agile grew, so grew an interest in automated software tools. Some legitimate reasons for this are as follows:

- Software tools provide a good way to help ensure data is captured in a consistent form.
- With consistently captured data, you can readily derive professional-looking reports, charts, and graphs.
- Providing history and safe storage is easy.
- You can instantly share the information with everyone no matter where they reside.
- With tools like online spreadsheets, you can even have a completely distributed team collaborate in real time.

Low-tech tools are a turn-off to some folks more accustomed to slick presentations and software. And since we are the industry that builds software, the natural inclination of many of us is to automate everything.

Bring on the software tools!

Eh...maybe not. Let's pause and think here. Automated tools may not support your team's specific process. Once you own a tool, the path of least resistance is to do whatever the tool provides regardless of whether it meets the team's needs.

Your team should establish the pattern of work compatible with their specific context first, and *then* consider using tools that support their workflow.

Workers use and control tools; tools don't control and use people.

You don't want to get locked into other people's process flows. Whatever you are doing, you want to get a handle on your process before you automate. The question, though, isn't whether to use automated or physical tools. The question should be "Are we using great tools or not-great tools?"

ALMs FOR THE NOT-POOR

Quickly after the onset of Agile, numerous software systems for managing Agile projects appeared. These Agile Lifecycle Management (ALM) systems, ranging from open source to polished and expensive "shrink-wrapped" products, allow you to collect Agile team data, manage long lists of features (backlogs), produce sophisticated graphs, provide cross-team summary views, and do some numerical processing.

It seems handy to have an automated system help us with this kind of work. In addition to their primary features, ALM tools have beneficial features: Most allow remote interaction, track history, handle some of the dirty-work bookkeeping, and are highly configurable. You can use a plotter to create professional, multicolor graphs on oversized paper that can be posted as information radiators in a team space.

Yet, despite being feature rich and commercially successful, ALM tools *utterly fail at being great*. This failure provides a good cautionary tale.

- *Great tools can be learned "well enough" quickly:* ALMs tend to be complicated, usually demanding up-front training. (Hmm. We're trying to remember the last index card training we attended.) Even with training, team members must often resort to searching the internet to figure out how to accomplish tasks that ought to be simple. Many acquiesce to the tool's complexity, punt on digging any deeper to figure things out, and end up tolerating slow, clunky ways of working.

- *Great tools become transparent to users.* We constantly see team members watching the designated driver trying to figure out the tool. They make seemingly drunken stabs at manipulating the story cards. They weave between web pages, slapping text about via copy-and-paste, trying to hook up stories with each other or to their parent "epics." They stumble over stories, tasks, and assignments in an attempt to make them all get along. It's a mess. These tools often require constant attention.

- *Great tools allow adaptation and exaptation.* Want to add fields to an ALM (virtual) card? You might be able to find a local programmer expert dedicated (sacrificed) to supporting the tool. Or you might end up having to submit a change request to the vendor. A five-second turn around time for low-tech tools turns into a five-day or five-week delay with an ALM. Rapid-feedback experiments around managing the process become impossible. And of course, if you don't need the extra fields after all, someone has to revert the changes and re-release the configuration. ALM tools aren't always easily adapted.

- *Great tools are affordable.* The ALM tool licensing fees, which can run into many thousands of dollars per year, are just the start. Installation and use of these tools can require additional considerable costs in the form of training, support, and sometimes customization. Ongoing maintenance and administration further add to the dear cost of ownership.

- *Great tools help people accomplish their objectives.* ALM tools rarely work the way your team does, and often their default mode is at odds with Agile methods. For example, many ALM tools assume that team members have individual work assignments, which makes them nearly unusable for teams who work together in a cross-functional way.

Some ALM tools even provide a *pillory board*—a dashboard showing each individual's workload, utilization, and progress (or lack thereof). Rather than highlighting the flow of work toward completion and promoting shared accountability—the truly Agile way—the tool becomes a weapon used to shame programmers into working harder and longer.

Where teams would gather for their morning standup (daily Scrum), they now gather to update their ALM. The tool has replaced interactions of individuals with automated status reporting.

Worst of all, ALM tools don't often radiate information like physical tools can. You have to log in and hunt around to find what you seek. When you do find the information, it often comes accompanied by a pile of other information you *don't* want. Sometimes the two or three graphs or displays you want are on different web pages.

There's no reason ALMs can't be great tools someday. But if you only need to manage a card wall and must use software, adopt a general-purpose tool like Trello.[8] It's easy, immediate, cheap, extensible, and won't make you queasy.

Our ways of working constantly change. We evolved from SCCS to RCS to CVS to Subversion to Git over the years, tracking a sea change in the ways we managed source code. We have similar evolution in testing tools, deployment tools, and the like (not listed here). We are likely to see a similar progression in automated ALM tools.

Given the current state of most ALM tools, it may be safer and smarter to begin with physical tools. Later, you can *consider* using an ALM tool. Make sure that it's quick to learn, transparent in daily use, easy to adapt, and within your means to acquire and run. Most importantly, ensure that it supports the way your team works and provides a positive return on your investment.

COACHING—AN ALTERNATIVE VIEW

By Damon Poole, May 14, 2019[*]

Damon Poole is a friend of mine who disagrees with me about many things. Agile coaching is just one of those things. So, I thought he'd make a good choice to provide you with a different viewpoint.

— UB

THE MANY PATHS TO AGILE

There are many paths to Agile. And in fact, many of us have walked the path unintentionally. One could argue that the Agile Manifesto was the result of the authors noticing that they were all on a similar journey and deciding to describe it such that others might choose to join them on their journey. My path to Agile started by walking into an appliance store in 1977 that happened to be selling TRS-80s. As a complete novice, I helped an

---

8. Again, as of 2019. The landscape changes.

* Used with permission.

experienced programmer debug a Star Trek game simply by asking questions. Today we call that Pair Programing. And, as it happens, asking questions is a big part of coaching.

From then until somewhere around 2001, I was unintentionally Agile. I only coded in small cross-functional teams, mostly with an in-house customer, focused on what are now called user stories, and we only produced small, frequent releases. But then, at AccuRev, our major releases started to get further and further apart, cresting at 18 months in 2005. For 4 years, I was unintentionally doing Waterfall development. It was horrible and I didn't know why. Moreover, I was considered a "process expert." Apart from the details, this is a familiar story for many people.

FROM PROCESS EXPERT TO AGILE EXPERT

My introduction to Agile was painful. Back in 2005, before the Agile Alliance conference and others skyrocketed in popularity, there were the *Software Development* magazine conferences. At the speaker reception for Software Development East, after doing a talk on management practices for distributed development that was completely devoid of the word "Agile," I found myself surrounded by software industry thought leaders such as Bob Martin, Joshua Kerievsky, Mike Cohn, and Scott Ambler. It seemed the only topics they had any passion for involved things like 3×5 cards, user stories, Test-Driven Development, and Pair Programming. I was horrified that all of these thought leaders had been taken in by what I saw as snake oil.

A few months later, while researching Agile in order to properly debunk it, I had an aha moment. As a programmer and business owner, this new insight came from understanding Agile as an algorithm for finding the highest-value-producing features in the market and then turning them into revenue faster.

After this moment of inspiration, I developed a passion for sharing Agile with everyone. I did free webinars, wrote blog posts, spoke at conferences, joined and then ran the Agile New England meetup in the Boston area, and did everything I could to spread the word. When people shared their difficulties in implementing Agile, I was brimming with enthusiasm to help. I launched into problem-solving mode and explained what I thought they should do.

I started to notice that my approach often led to objections and more questions. And it wasn't just me. On the extreme end, I witnessed multiple Agilists in conference sessions becoming confrontational with those that had not yet seen the light. I began to realize that for people to really embrace and utilize Agile effectively, there needed to be another way to impart Agile knowledge and experience that took into account the learner's unique circumstances.

THE NEED FOR AGILE COACHING

The concept of Agile is simple. It is described in a mere 264 words in the Agile Manifesto. But becoming Agile is hard. If it was easy, everybody would already be doing it and there would be no need for Agile coaches. People have a hard time making changes in general, let alone the amount of change it takes to fully embrace Agile. Becoming Agile involves revisiting entrenched beliefs, culture, process, thinking, and ways of working. Getting one person to shift thinking and help them see "what's in it for me" is challenging enough. Doing that for a whole team compounds the difficulty, and when it takes place within an environment that is purpose built for traditional ways of working, the difficulty is compounded again.

A truism of all change initiatives is that people do what they want to do. The key to lasting change is to find problems or opportunities that people are aware of and have a desire to invest in and then help them achieve their goals, offering expertise only as requested and needed. Everything else will fail. Coaching helps people discover the blind spots and surface the underlying beliefs that keep them from moving forward. It helps people to solve their own challenges and reach their own goals rather than just prescribing a solution.

PUTTING THE COACH INTO AGILE COACH

In 2008, Lyssa Adkins came on the scene with a very different approach to Agile coaching. She put an emphasis on the pure coaching aspect of Agile coaching by introducing skills from professional coaching into the Agile coaching world.

As I learned more about professional coaching and Lyssa's approach and started to incorporate it into my own way of working, I came to understand that people get a tremendous amount of value out of the process of coaching itself. That value is completely separate from any increase in Agile knowledge or expertise that a coach may also impart to them.

In 2010, Lyssa fully described her approach to Agile coaching in her book *Coaching Agile Teams*.[9] At the same time, she started offering an Agile coaching course. In 2011, those learning objectives formed the basis of ICAgile's Certified Agile Coach (ICP-ACC) learning objectives and International Consortium for Agile then began accrediting other instructors with their own ICP-ACC offerings. ICP-ACC courses are currently the most comprehensive source of professional coaching instruction in the Agile industry.

GOING BEYOND THE ICP-ACC

The ICP-ACC certification includes the coaching skills of active listening, emotional intelligence, presence, providing clear and direct feedback, asking open-ended and non-leading questions, and remaining neutral. The full set of professional coaching skills is even broader. For instance, the International Coach Federation (ICF), representing more than 35,000 certified professional coaches, defines 70 competencies organized into 11 categories. Becoming a certified professional coach involves a great deal of training and a rigorous certification process that requires demonstrating all 70 competencies and documenting hundreds of hours of paid coaching.

---

9. Adkins, L. 2010. *Coaching Agile Teams: A Companion for ScrumMasters, Agile Coaches, and Project Managers in Transition.* Boston, MA: Addison-Wesley.

COACHING TOOLS

Many of the structures, practices, methods, and techniques used in the Agile community for teaching Agile and being Agile align with the intent of professional coaching. They are "coaching tools" that help individuals and groups discover for themselves what's getting in their way and decide on their own how to move forward.

One coaching competency is *powerful questioning,* one aspect of which is "asking questions that evoke discovery, insight, commitment, or action." Retrospectives, especially variants like "Team with the Best Results Ever" or "Six Hats" are a way to ask powerful questions that enable a team to discover opportunities for change on their own and decide independently how to go about pursuing those opportunities. An open space (aka *unconference*) is a way to ask a powerful question of a large group of people, even a whole organization.

If you have taken formal training on Agile or an Agile methodology, you likely played a number of games that illustrated Agile concepts. Games such as the penny game, Scrum simulations, Kanban Pizza, or LEGO city building. These games give participants an experiential connection to the power of self-organization, small batch sizes, cross-functional teams, TDD, Scrum, and Kanban. When the games are run with the intent of raising participants' awareness and then letting participants decide what to do next, they capture the spirit of professional coaching.

There is a growing body of coaching tools. Many of them can be found at tastycupcakes.org, retromat.org, and liberatingstructures.com.

PROFESSIONAL COACHING SKILLS ARE NOT ENOUGH

If we are working with a team that has never heard of Kanban but may benefit from it, no amount of powerful questions or other professional coaching techniques are going to result in someone spontaneously inventing Kanban. At that point, an Agile coach switches to a mode of offering potentially useful expertise. If the team is interested, the Agile coach then provides their expertise, teaching and mentoring the team with the intention of moving back to pure coaching as soon as the team has mastered the new knowledge.

There are six main areas of expertise that Agile coaches draw from: Agile frameworks, Agile transformation, Agile product management, Agile technical practices, facilitation, and coaching. Each coach will have her own mix of skills. Most organizations start by looking for an Agile coach that has Agile framework experience. As companies progress in their journey, they come to appreciate the value of each area of Agile expertise.

One area of expertise that organizations consistently underestimate is the need for everyone involved in coding and testing to get good at writing code and creating tests that are appropriate for an Agile environment as described elsewhere in this book. This is important to keep the focus on adding new functionality with new tests rather than constantly updating existing code and tests and/or increasing technical debt, both of which add an increasing drag on velocity.

Coaching in a Multiteam Environment

Somewhere around 2012, as more organizations had success with individual teams, there was a huge uptick in interest in *scaling* Agile. That is, transforming the organization from being purpose built for traditional ways of working to one that is purpose built to support Agile ways of working.

These days, most Agile coaching happens within the context of multiple teams, sometimes tens or hundreds of teams. And it frequently starts with resources (people) siloed and allocated to three or more unrelated projects. Not all of those "teams" are working together toward a common purpose, but they are all working within a traditional environment that thinks in terms of multiyear funding, portfolio planning, and project-based thinking rather than team- and product-based thinking.

AGILE IN THE LARGE

Agile in the large is a very similar problem to Agile at the team level. Part of the difficulty of getting the benefit of Agile is finding and removing all of the obstacles that get in the way of a team coordinating their efforts to go from request to ready for release in the span of a couple of weeks. It is even harder to get a team to the point of releasing on demand.

These difficulties are multiplied and magnified when trying to coordinate the efforts of multiple teams to produce a single deliverable. Unfortunately, a common pattern of Agile adoption in large organizations is to treat the adoption like a traditional project. That is, a top-down command and control rollout of a huge number of changes decided on as part of an up-front design. And when I say huge, I mean literally thousands of changes. It is in the thousands because when you ask hundreds of people to make dozens of changes to their day-to-day behavior, each of those have a chance to succeed or fail based on how each of those hundreds of people feels about the impact on them personally. Starting out by saying that a large Agile framework is your destination sounds very similar to saying, "Our plan is to implement this large stack of software requirements."

In my experience working with many large Agile adoptions (many with hundreds of teams) and working alongside many experienced Agile coaches, the most important thing I've learned is this: the problem of successfully adopting Agile is exactly the same problem as creating successful software. Just as it is best to grow your software based on frequent customer interaction, the only process changes that will stick are those that are directly connected to what the people affected understand and desire based on their own unique circumstances. In other words, I believe that the most effective Agile transformation strategy is to treat the introduction of Agile as an Agile endeavor, applied using coaching skills.

USING AGILE AND COACHING TO BECOME AGILE

The Agile Manifesto is a great template for coaching and coordinating the work of multiple teams: "Give them the environment and support they need, and trust them to get the job done." In support of this, the Agile community has a whole host of scaling patterns that are compatible with the values and principles of the Agile Manifesto. I am not referring to frameworks here, but rather the individual practices from which all of the frameworks are built.

All of the frameworks are basically "ready-made" recipes composed of individual Agile practices. Rather than implementing one of these recipes, consider using Agile and coaching to discover and implement a custom recipe that is tailor-made to your specific circumstances. If, in the end, that recipe ends up being SAFe, Nexus, LeSS, or Scrum@Scale, that's great!

Here is an overview of how the most successful enterprise Agile coaches combine Agile and coaching to discover and implement Agile in a way that is perfect for the organization. The essence of coaching at the individual level is helping people solve problems on their own. Coaching at the team and organizational levels means helping teams achieve their goals on their own. First, the coach thinks of everyone affected by the Agile adoption as "the customers." Then, using retrospectives, open-space events, and similar techniques, they discover what the customers see as the challenges and opportunities. This becomes the organization's Agile adoption backlog. Next, using group decision-making tools such as dot voting, the coach determines the top of the backlog. They then assist the organization to implement a handful of the top backlog items. Finally, they retrospect and repeat.
Of course, for many of the people involved, this will be their first Agile adoption. Coaching alone is not enough; teaching and mentoring will also come into play so that people will be able to make informed decisions.

GROWING YOUR AGILE ADOPTION

Here is a list of individual practices to consider for your Agile adoption backlog. This list was originally created and has been periodically updated by the Agile coaching trifecta of gathering sticky notes, de-duping, and dot voting with a group of a dozen or so enterprise coaches. This is just a high-level description of these practices for reference. There are many more Agile practices out there—consider this a starting place. For instance, rather than adopting Scrum, Kanban, XP, or one of the scaling frameworks, consider which single practice from the list below is most relevant to a current need for a defined group or team, and adopt that. Try it for a while, then repeat.

- **The practices of Kanban**—Kanban practices include making the work visible (via a card wall), limiting work in progress, and pulling work through the system.

- **The practices of Scrum and XP**—These two methodologies are grouped together because they are very similar apart from the technical practices in XP. In SAFe, for instance, they are referred to collectively as *ScrumXP*. Between the two of them, they include a wide variety of practices such as short daily team meetings, a product owner, a process facilitator (aka Scrum Master), retrospectives, a cross-functional team, user stories, small releases, refactoring, writing tests first, and pair programming.

- **Align team events**—When the team events across multiple teams, such as standups and retrospectives, are aligned in time, it is possible to then roll up daily and systemic impediments via an escalation tree. This involves aligning iteration start and stop times as well as iteration length. Teams that don't use iterations and are able to release on demand can align with any other cadence.

- **Escalation trees**—If it makes sense to always work on items that produce the highest value, then it makes sense to escalate impediments immediately via a well-defined escalation path. This applies to the commonly used practice of "Scrum of Scrums" and the less well-known "retrospective of retrospectives." One pattern for this is Scrum@Scale's fractal pattern of scaling via Scrum and Scrum of Scrums backstopped with an Executive Action Team.

- **Regular interteam interaction**—This practice involves regular interaction between the Scrum Masters, Product Owners, and team members who are working together toward a common deliverable. One method for this is to run regular open-space events.

- **Portfolio Kanban**—Traditional portfolio management practices tend to allocate people to multiple teams, which leads to rampant multitasking. Multitasking creates friction, increases complexity, and reduces throughput. Portfolio Kanban sets work in progress limits at the initiative level in order to ensure that the organization is focused on the highest-value work at all times. Having fewer projects in progress at a time also vastly simplifies (or even eliminates) multiteam coordination. Portfolio Kanban works best when paired with Minimum Viable Increments.

- **Minimum Viable Increments**—There are many variants of this idea, but they all boil down to thinking about what is the shortest path to producing the highest value in the shortest time. A growing number of organizations are taking this to the extreme by implementing Continuous Delivery: releasing small updates on a frequent basis, sometimes as frequently as multiple times per day.

GOING BIG BY FOCUSING ON THE SMALL

Most multiteam Agile adoptions run into problems when they focus on coping with complexity rather than solving for simplicity. In my experience, one of the cornerstones of Agility in the large is very high levels of Agility at the team level and very low levels of complexity everywhere. Having a flotilla of speedboats is nearly useless if they are all joined together. Here are some of the practices that are generally associated with team-level Agile that do double duty as enablers of multiteam coordination.

- **The SOLID principles**—Although these principles are valuable at any scale, they are especially useful for simplifying multiteam coordination by dramatically reducing dependencies.
- **Small, valuable user stories**—Small, individually releasable stories limit the scope of dependencies, which simplifies multiteam coordination.
- **Small, frequent releases**—Whether these releases are delivered to the customer or not, the practice of having a releasable product across all of the teams involved helps to surface coordination and architectural issues so that the root cause can be found and addressed. Some Scrum teams forget this, but Scrum says, "The increment must be in useable condition regardless of whether the Product Owner decides to release it." That means it must be integrated with the work of any other teams that it depends on.
- **Continuous Integration**—XP takes an even stronger stand on integration, calling for integration across the entire product after every checkin.

- **Simple Design**—This practice, also known as Emergent Design, is one of the hardest practices to learn and apply because it is one of the most counter-intuitive practices. Teams struggle with this even when they don't need to coordinate with other teams. When coordinating the work of multiple teams, monolithic, centralized, preplanned architectures create massive dependencies between teams that tend to force them to work in lock step, thus defeating much of the promise of Agile. Simple Design, especially when used with practices such as a microservices architecture, enables Agility in the large.

THE FUTURE OF AGILE COACHING

In the last few years, professional coaching and professional facilitation have started to make their way into the Agile curriculum. The Scrum Alliance's Advanced Certified Scrum Master (ACSM) course has a few learning objectives related to coaching and facilitation, and their Certified Team Coach (CTC) and Certified Enterprise Coach (CEC) programs require that you acquire even more facilitation and coaching skills than that. The Scrum guide now refers to Scrum Masters as coaching those they serve.

As more people are exposed to professional coaching through the courses mentioned above and through interaction with professional coaches working in the Agile community, the "coach" part of Agile coach is getting more attention. In the last couple of months, it seems that the interest in professional coaching has blossomed. People have started skipping the ICP-ACC path in favor of going directly to the ICF path. The first ICF-credentialed coaching school that caters to Agilists has been formed, and there's at least one more on the way. The future of Agile coaching is bright!

CONCLUSION (BOB AGAIN)

In many ways, this chapter has been more about what *not* to do than what to do. Perhaps that's because I've seen so many examples of how *not* to become Agile. After all, I still think, as I thought 20 years ago, "What could be easier? Just follow a few simple disciplines and practices. Nothing to it."

7 CRAFTSMANSHIP

By Sandro Mancuso, April 27, 2019

Excitement. That's what many developers felt when they first heard about Agile. For most of us, developers coming from the software factories and Waterfall mentality, Agile was the hope for emancipation. It was the hope that we would work in a collaborative environment and that our opinions would be listened to and respected. We would have better working processes and practices. We would be working in small iterations and short feedback loops. We would release our application to production regularly. We would interact with users and get their feedback. We would constantly inspect and adapt our ways of working. We would be involved at the beginning of the process. We would have daily contact with the business. In fact, we would be a single team. We would regularly discuss business and technical challenges and together agree on a way forward, and we would be treated as professionals. Business and technology would work together to produce great software products, delivering value to our companies and clients.

At the beginning, we felt Agile was too good to be true. We thought our companies would never embrace the Agile mindset, let alone the Agile practices. But most of them did, and we were positively surprised. Suddenly, everything was different. We had product backlogs and user stories instead of requirement documents. We had physical boards and burn-down charts instead of Gantt charts. We had sticky notes that we moved every morning according to our progress. There was something powerful about those sticky notes—something that provoked a deep psychological addiction. They were the representation of our *agility*. The more sticky notes we had on the walls, the more "Agile" we felt we were. We became a Scrum team instead of a construction team. And we didn't have project managers anymore. We were told we did not need to be managed; our managers would now be product owners, and we would self-organize. We were told that product owners and developers would work in close collaboration, as a single team. And from now on, as the Scrum team, we were empowered to make decisions—not only technical decisions, but project-related decisions. Or so we thought.

Agile took the software industry by storm. But as in a Chinese whispers game, the original Agile ideas got distorted and simplified, arriving at companies as the promise of *a process to deliver software faster*. For companies and managers using Waterfall or RUP, that was music to their ears.

Managers and stakeholders were excited. At the end of the day, who would not want to be Agile? Who would not want to deliver software faster? Even among the skeptical, Agile could not be rejected. If your competitors are advertising that they are Agile, but you are not, what does it make you? What would your potential customers think about you? Companies could not afford not to be Agile. And in the years that followed the Agile summit, companies all over the world embarked on their Agile transformation. The Agile Transformation Era had begun.

THE AGILE HANGOVER

Transitioning from one culture to another was not easy. Companies needed external help to transform their organization and a huge demand for a new type of professional emerged: Agile coaches. Many Agile certification schemes were created. Some certifications could be obtained by simply attending a two-day training course.

Selling Agile processes to middle managers was an easy sell—they all wanted software to be delivered faster. "Engineering is the easy part. If we fix the process, engineering will be fixed," managers were told. "It's always a people problem." And they bought it. Managers manage people, and as long as they are in charge, they are happy to have their direct reports working faster.

Many companies truly benefited from their Agile transformation, and today they are in a much better place than they were before. Many of these companies can deploy software to production multiple times a day and have business and technology truly working as a single team. But that is certainly not true for many others. Managers willing to push developers to work faster are using the full transparency of the process to micromanage them. Agile coaches with neither business nor technical experience are coaching *managers* and telling development teams what to do. Roadmaps and milestones are being defined by managers and forced upon development teams—developers can estimate the work, but they are pushed hard to fit their estimates into the imposed milestones. It is fairly common to see projects that have all their iterations and respective user stories already defined by management for the next 6 to 12 months. Failing to deliver all story points in a sprint means developers must work harder in the next sprint to make up for the delay. Daily standup meetings become meetings where developers must report progress to product owners and Agile coaches, detailing what they are working on and when they will be done. If the product owner thinks developers are spending too much time on things like automated tests, refactoring, or pairing, they simply tell the team to stop doing it.

Strategic technical work has no place in *their* Agile process. There is no need for architecture or design. The order is to simply focus on the highest-priority item in the backlog and get it done as fast as possible—one highest-priority item after another. This approach results in a long sequence of iterative tactical work and accumulation of technical debt. Fragile software, the famous monoliths (or distributed monoliths for the teams trying micro services) become the norm. Bugs and operational problems are popular discussion topics during daily standup meetings and retrospectives. Releases to production are not as frequent as the business expected. Manual testing cycles still take days, if not weeks, to complete. And the hope that adopting Agile would prevent all these issues is gone. Managers blame developers for not moving quickly enough. Developers blame managers for not allowing them to do the technical and strategic work needed. Product owners do not consider themselves as part of the team and do not share the responsibility when things go wrong. The us-versus-them culture reigns dominant.

That is what we call the *Agile Hangover*. After years of investment in an Agile transformation, companies realized that they still have many of the problems they had before. And Agile is being blamed for that, of course.

EXPECTATION MISMATCH

Agile transformations that purely focus on process are partial transformations. While Agile coaches try to guide managers and delivery teams through the Agile processes, there is no one helping developers learn Agile technical practices and engineering. The assumption that fixing the collaboration among people would improve engineering could not be more wrong.

Good collaboration removes some of the blocks people have to do their jobs but does not necessarily make them more skilled.

There is a big expectation that comes with Agile adoption: development teams should deliver production-ready software as soon as a feature is done, or at the least at the end of each iteration. For most development teams, that is a significant change. There is no way they can achieve that without changing the way they work, and that means learning and mastering new practices. But there are a few problems. Rarely is there a budget for up-skilling developers during Agile transformations. Business does not expect developers to slow down during their Agile adoption. Most do not even know developers have to learn new practices. They were told that if they worked in a more collaborative way, developers would work faster.

Releasing software to production every two weeks requires a lot of discipline and technical skills—skills that are not commonly found in teams used to delivering software a few times per year. Things get much worse when multiple teams, with quite a few developers each, all working on the same systems, are expected to deliver features to production as they finish them. The level of mastery in technical practices and engineering must be extremely high for teams to deploy software to production multiple times a day without compromising the overall stability of the system. Developers cannot just pick an item from the top of a product backlog, start coding, and think that everything is going to be OK when they push to production. They need strategic thinking. They need a modular design that supports parallel work. They need to continuously embrace change while making sure the system can always be deployed to production. For that, they need to continuously build software that is both flexible and robust. But balancing flexibility and robustness with the need to deploy software to production continuously is extremely hard and cannot be done without the necessary engineering skills.

It is not realistic to think that teams will develop these skills simply by creating a more collaborative environment. Teams need support in acquiring these technical skills. This support can happen through a combination of coaching, training, experimentation, and self-learning. Business agility is directly related to how quickly companies can evolve their software, and that means an evolution in their engineering skills and technical practices.

MOVING APART

Of course, not every Agile transformation or company suffers from all the problems described earlier, or at least not to the same degree. In terms of business, it is fair to say that most companies that have gone through an Agile transformation, even if partially, are in a better place today. They are working in shorter iterations. The collaboration between business and technology is closer than it was before. Problems and risks are being identified earlier. Businesses are reacting faster as they get new information, truly benefiting from an iterative approach to software development. However, although companies are indeed better than they were before, the split between Agile processes and engineering are still hurting them. Most modern Agile coaches do not have enough (if any) technical skills to coach developers on technical practices, and they rarely talk about engineering. Over the years, developers started seeing Agile coaches as another layer of management: people telling them what to do instead of helping them to get better at what they do.

Are developers moving away from Agile, or is Agile moving away from developers?

The answer to this question is probably both. It seems that Agile and developers are moving away from each other. In many organizations, Agile has become synonymous with Scrum. XP, when present, is reduced to a few technical practices like TDD and Continuous Integration. There is an expectation from Agile coaches that developers apply some of the XP practices, but they do not really help or get involved in the way developers are working. Many Product Owners (or project managers) still do not feel they are part of the team and do not feel responsible when things do not go according to plan. Developers still need to negotiate hard with the business to make the necessary technical improvements to keep developing and maintaining the system.

Companies are still not mature enough to understand that technical problems are in fact business problems.

With a diminishing focus on technical skills, can Agile significantly improve software projects beyond what it did up until now? Is Agile still focused on *uncovering better ways of developing software by doing it and helping others do it,* as it was written in the Agile Manifesto? I'm not so sure.

SOFTWARE CRAFTSMANSHIP

To raise the bar of professional software development and re-establish some of the original Agile goals, a group of developers met in November 2008 in Chicago to create a new movement: Software Craftsmanship. In that meeting, similar to what happened during the Agile summit in 2001, they agreed on a core set of values and came up with a new manifesto[1] that was built on top of the Agile Manifesto:

As aspiring Software Craftsmen, we are raising the bar of professional software development by practicing it and helping others learn the craft. Through this work we have come to value:

- Not only working software, but also **well-crafted software**
- Not only responding to change, but also **steadily adding value**
- Not only individuals and interactions, but also **a community of professionals**
- Not only customer collaboration, but also **productive partnerships**

That is, in pursuit of the items on the left we have found the items on the right to be indispensable.

The Software Craftsmanship manifesto describes an ideology, a mindset. It promotes professionalism through different perspectives.

Well-crafted software means code that is well designed and well tested. It is code that we are not scared to change and code that enables business to react fast. It is code that is both flexible and robust.

Steadily adding value means that no matter what we do, we should always be committed to continuously provide increasing value to our clients and employers.

A community of professionals means that we are expected to share and learn with each other, raising the bar of our industry. We are responsible for preparing the next generation of developers.

---

1. http://manifesto.softwarecraftsmanship.org

Productive partnerships means we will have a professional relationship with our clients and employers. We will always behave ethically and respectfully, advising and working with our clients and employers in the best way possible. We will expect a relationship of mutual respect and professionalism even if we need to take the initiative and lead by example.

We will look at our work not as something we need to do as part of a job but as a professional service we provide. We will take ownership of our own careers, investing our own time and money to get better at what we do. These values are not only professional values—they are personal values. Craftspeople strive to do the best job they can, not because someone is paying, but based on a desire to do things well.

Thousands of developers across the world immediately subscribed to the principles and values espoused by Software Craftsmanship. The original excitement that developers felt in the early days of Agile was not only back, but also stronger. Craftspeople, as they started calling themselves, decided not to let their movement be hijacked again. It is a developers' movement. A movement that inspires developers to be the best they can be. A movement that inspires developers to become and see themselves as highly skilled professionals.

IDEOLOGY VERSUS METHODOLOGY

An ideology is a system of ideas and ideals. A methodology is a system of methods and practices. An ideology defines ideals to be aimed at. One or more methodologies can be used to reach those ideals—they are a means to an end. When looking at the Agile Manifesto and the 12 principles,[2] we can clearly see the ideology behind them. The main goal of Agile is to provide business agility and customer satisfaction, and that is achieved via close collaboration, iterative development, short feedback loops, and technical excellence. Methodologies like Scrum, Extreme Programming (XP), Dynamic Systems Development Method (DSDM), Adaptive Software Development

---

2. https://agilemanifesto.org/principles.html

(ASD), Crystal Methods, Feature-Driven Development (FDD), and other Agile methodologies are all means to the same end.

Methodologies and practices are like training wheels; they are great to get people started. As with children learning to ride a bicycle, the training wheels allow them to get started in a safe and controlled way. Once they are a bit more confident, we raise the training wheels a bit so they can practice their equilibrium. We then take one of the training wheels off. And then the other. At this point, the child is ready to go on his own. But if we focus too much on the importance of the training wheels and keep them on for too long, the child gets too dependent on them and does not want them to be removed. The obsessive focus on a methodology or set of practices distracts teams and organizations from their real goals. The goal is to teach a child to ride a bicycle, not to adopt the training wheels.

In his book *Agile Project Management: Creating Innovative Products,* Jim Highsmith says, "Principles without practices are empty shells, whereas practices without principles tend to be implemented by rote, without judgement. Principles guide practices. Practices instantiate principles. They go hand in hand."[3] Although methodologies and practices are a means to an end, we should not deemphasize their importance. Professionals are defined by the way they work. We cannot claim to have certain principles and values when our ways of working (methods and practices) are not aligned to them. Good professionals can precisely describe how they work given a specific context. They master a wide set of practices and are able to use them according to their needs.

DOES SOFTWARE CRAFTSMANSHIP HAVE PRACTICES?

Software Craftsmanship does not have practices. Rather, it promotes a perpetual search for better practices and ways of working. Good practices are good until we discover better ones to replace them. Attaching specific practices to Software Craftsmanship would make it weak and obsolete as

---

3. Highsmith, J. 2009. *Agile Project Management: Creating Innovative Products,* 2nd ed. Boston, MA: Addison-Wesley, 85.

better practices are discovered. But that does not mean that the international Software Craftsmanship community does not advocate any practices. On the contrary, since its creation in 2008, the Software Craftsmanship community considers XP the best set of Agile development practices currently available. TDD, Refactoring, Simple Design, Continuous Integration, and Pair Programming are heavily advocated by the Software Craftsmanship community—but they are XP practices, not Craftsmanship practices. And they are not the only practices. Craftsmanship also promotes Clean Code and SOLID principles. It promotes small commits, small releases, and Continuous Delivery. It promotes modularity in software design and any type of automation that removes manual and repetitive work. And it promotes any practices that improve productivity, reduce risk, and help to produce valuable, robust, and flexible software.

Craftsmanship is not only about technical practices, engineering, and self-improvement. It is also about professionalism and enabling clients to achieve their business goals. And this is an area where Agile, Lean, and Craftsmanship are in perfect alignment. All three have similar goals but tackle the problem from different but equally important and complementary perspectives.

FOCUS ON THE VALUE, NOT THE PRACTICE

A common mistake in the Agile and Craftsmanship communities is to promote practices instead of the value they provide. Let's take TDD as an example. One of the most common questions asked inside the Craftsmanship communities is "How do I convince my manager/colleague/team to do TDD?" That is the wrong question. The problem here is that we are offering a solution before agreeing on the problem. People will not change the way they work if they do not see the value.

Instead of pushing TDD, maybe we could start agreeing on the value of reducing the time it takes to test our entire system. How long does it take today? Two hours? Two days? Two weeks? How many people are involved? What if we could reduce it to 20 minutes? Two minutes? Maybe even

2 seconds? And what if we could do that at any time just by pressing a button? Would that give us a good return on investment? Would that make our lives easier? Would we be able to release reliable software faster?

If we agree that the answer is yes, then we can start talking about practices which could help us achieve that. TDD would be a natural choice here. For those who are not so keen on TDD, we should ask what practice they would prefer. What practice can they suggest that could bring the same or higher value according to the agreed-upon goals?

Agreeing first on the goals to be achieved is essential when discussing practices. The only thing that should not be acceptable is to reject a practice without providing a better alternative.

DISCUSSING PRACTICES

The discussion around practices should be done at the right level and with the right people. If we want to adopt practices that improve the collaboration between business and technology, people from business and technology should be involved in the discussion. If developers are discussing practices that would enable them to build systems in a better way, there is no reason to involve businesspeople. Business should only be involved when there is a significant impact in the cost or duration of the project.

There is a difference between re-architecting a whole monolith system into microservices and doing TDD. The former has a very significant impact on the cost and duration of the project; the latter doesn't, as long as developers are comfortable with the technique. Whether or not developers automate their tests should not be relevant to the business. It should be even less relevant whether the automated tests are written before or after the production code. What business should care about is that the lead time from business ideas to software in production is gradually reduced. Reducing the amount of money and time spent on rework (bugs, manual processes like testing, deployment, and production monitoring) is also a business concern that should be addressed by the development teams. Reducing the cost of experimenting is also a business concern. Experimenting becomes very costly when the software is not modular and easily testable. Business and developers should have conversations about business value, not technical practices.

Developers should not ask authorization for writing tests. They should not have separate tasks for unit tests or refactoring. They should not have separate tasks for making a feature production ready. These technical activities should be factored into the development of any feature. They are not optional. Managers and developers should only discuss what is going to be delivered and when, not how. Every time developers volunteer details of how they work, they are inviting managers to micromanage them.

Are we saying that developers should hide how they work? No, not at all. Developers should be able to clearly describe how they work and the advantages of working that way to whomever is interested. What developers should not do is to let other people decide how they work. Conversations between developers and business should be about why, what, and when—not how.

CRAFTSMANSHIP IMPACT ON INDIVIDUALS

Craftsmanship has a profound impact on individuals. It is common to see people separating their personal lives from their professional lives. Phrases like "I do not want to talk about work after I leave the office," or "I have different interests in life" are said in a way that makes work look like a chore, a bad thing, or a thing you do because you have to, not because you want to. The problem of dividing our lives into multiple lives is that they are constantly in conflict. There is always that feeling that we must sacrifice one life for the sake of the other, regardless of which life we pick.

Craftsmanship promotes software development as a profession. There is a difference between having a job and having a profession. A job is a thing we do but it is not part of who we are. A profession, on the other hand, is part of who we are. When asked, "What do you do?", a person with a job would normally say something like "I *work for* company X," or "I *work as* a software developer." But a person with a profession would generally say, "I *am* a software developer." A profession is something we invest in. It's something we want to get better at. We want to gain more skills and have a long-lasting and fulfilling career.

That does not mean we would not spend time with our families or that we would not have other interests in life. Rather, it means that we would find a way to balance all our commitments and interests such that we can live a single, well-balanced, and happy life. There are times when we want to give more attention to our family, our profession, or a hobby we might have. And that is totally OK. We have different needs at different times. But going to work should not be a chore when we have a profession. It is just another thing we do that gives us pleasure and fulfills us as individuals. A profession gives meaning to our lives.

CRAFTSMANSHIP IMPACT ON OUR INDUSTRY

Since 2008, a growing number of Software Craftsmanship communities and conferences are being organized all over the world, attracting tens of thousands of developers. While Agile communities have an emphasis on the people and process side of software projects, the Craftsmanship communities focus more on the technical side. They have been key in promoting XP, and many other technical practices to many developers and companies around the world. It is through Software Craftsmanship communities that many developers are learning TDD, Continuous Integration, Pair Programming, Simple Design, SOLID principles, Clean Code, and Refactoring. They are also learning how to architect systems using microservices, how to automate their deployment pipelines, and how to migrate their systems to the cloud. They are learning different programming languages and paradigms. They are learning new technologies and different ways to test and maintain their applications. Developers in the Craftsmanship community are creating safe and friendly spaces where they can meet like-minded people and talk about their profession.

Software Craftsmanship communities are extremely inclusive. From the very beginning, one of the main goals of Software Craftsmanship was to bring together software developers from all backgrounds so that they could learn from each other and raise the bar of professional software development. Craftsmanship communities are technology agnostic, and all developers, regardless of their level of experience, are welcome in the meetings. The community is committed to preparing the next generation of professionals, creating various events where people joining our industry can learn essential practices to build well-crafted software.

CRAFTSMANSHIP IMPACT ON COMPANIES

Software Craftsmanship adoption is growing. Many companies that have adopted Agile are now looking at Craftsmanship to improve their engineering capabilities. However, Software Craftsmanship does not have the same business appeal that Agile has. XP is still something that many managers do not understand or are excited about. Managers understand Scrum, iterations, demos, retrospectives, collaboration, and a fast feedback loop. But they are not so interested in programming-related techniques. For most of them, XP is about programming, not about Agile software development.

Differently from Agile coaches in the early 2000s, who had a strong technical background, most Agile coaches today cannot teach XP practices or talk to businesspeople about engineering. They cannot sit down with developers and Pair Program with them. They cannot talk about Simple Design or help with the configuration of Continuous Integration pipelines. They cannot help developers to refactor their legacy code. They can discuss neither testing strategies nor how to maintain multiple services in production. They cannot explain to businesspeople the real advantages of certain technical practices, let alone create or advise on a technical strategy.

But companies need reliable systems—systems that enable them to react quickly according to their business needs. Companies also need motivated and capable technical teams that can do a great job creating and maintaining their systems. And those are areas where Software Craftsmanship excels.

The Software Craftsmanship mindset is an inspiration for many developers. It gives them a sense of purpose, a sense of pride, and an innate willingness to do things well. Most developers, as people in general, are keen to learn and do things well—they just need support and an environment where they can thrive. Companies embracing Craftsmanship often see internal communities of practice flourish. Developers organize internal sessions where they code together, practice TDD, and improve their software design skills. They become interested in learning new technologies and modernizing the systems they work on. They discuss better ways to improve the codebase and eliminate technical debit. Software Craftsmanship promotes a culture of learning, making companies more innovative and responsive.

CRAFTSMANSHIP AND AGILE

Some of the triggers for the creation of the Software Craftsmanship movement were related to the frustration that many developers felt with the direction Agile had taken. Because of that, some people felt that Craftsmanship and Agile were at odds with each other. People in the Craftsmanship movement who had also been part of the Agile movement criticized Agile for their excessive focus on process and lack of focus on engineering. People in the Agile movement criticized Craftsmanship for its narrow focus or lack of focus on *real* business and people problems.

Although there were some valid concerns coming from both sides, most of the disagreements were more related to tribalism than actual fundamental divergence of opinions. Essentially, both movements want to achieve very similar things. They both want customer satisfaction, they both desire close collaboration, and they both value short feedback loops. Both want to deliver high-quality, valuable work, and both want *professionalism*. In order to achieve business agility, companies need not only collaborative and iterative processes, but also good engineering skills. Combining Agile and Craftsmanship is the perfect way to achieve that.

CONCLUSION

At the Snowbird meeting in 2001, Kent Beck said that Agile was about the healing of the divide between development and business. Unfortunately, as the project managers flooded into the Agile community, the developers—who had created the Agile community in the first place—felt dispossessed and undervalued. So, they left to form the Craftsmanship movement. Thus, the ancient distrust continues.

And yet the values of Agile and the values of Craftsmanship are strongly aligned. These two movements should not be separate. One hopes that, one day, they'll come together again.

CONCLUSION

So, that's it. Those are my memories, my opinions, and my rantings and ravings about Agile. I hope you enjoyed them and maybe even learned a thing or two.

Agile may be the most significant, and most persistent, of all the revolutions we have seen about software processes and methods. That significance and persistence are evidence that those 17 folks who went to Snowbird, Utah, during February 2001 started a snowball rolling down a very long hill. Riding that snowball, watching it gather size and speed, and seeing it hit boulders and trees has been a load of fun for me.

I wrote this book because I thought it was time for someone to stand up and yell about what Agile was and what Agile still ought to be. I thought it was time to remember the basics.

Those basics were, are, and will be the disciplines in Ron Jeffries' Circle of Life. Those basics are the values, principles, and disciplines of Kent Beck's *Extreme Programming Explained*.[1] Those basics are the motivations, techniques, and disciplines in Martin Fowler's *Refactoring*.[2] Those basics were stated by Booch, DeMarco, Yourdon, Constantine, Page-Jones, and Lister.

---

1. Beck, K. 2000. *Extreme Programming Explained: Embrace Change*. Boston, MA: Addison-Wesley.
2. Fowler, M. 2019. *Refactoring: Improving the Design of Existing Code*, 2nd ed. Boston, MA: Addison-Wesley.

They were shouted by Dijkstra, Dahl, and Hoare. You heard them from Knuth, Meyer, Jacobsen, and Rumbaugh. And they were echoed by Coplien, Gamma, Helm, Vlissides, and Johnson. If you listened carefully, you'd have heard them whispered by Thompson, Ritchie, Kernighan, and Plauger. And—somewhere—Church, von Neumann, and Turing all smiled as those echoes and whispers went by.

Those basics are old, tried, and true. No matter how much new fluff is added around the edges, those basics are still there, still relevant, and still the core of Agile software development.

AFTERWORD

By Eric Crichlow, April 5, 2019

I can easily recall the first job I had where they decided to transition to Agile. That was in 2008 at a company that had been acquired by a larger corporation. It was undergoing significant changes to its policies, procedures, and personnel. I can also remember a couple of other jobs where an emphasis was placed on Agile practices. The rituals were followed religiously: sprint planning, demo, sprint review... At one of them, every developer in the company was put through two days of Agile training with a certified Scrum Master. As a mobile developer, they had me write a mobile app for playing Agile Poker.

But in the 11 years since my first exposure to Agile, I have also been at several companies where I honestly can't remember whether they used Agile practices. Maybe that's because Agile has become so ubiquitous that it's easy to take it for granted and not even think about it. Or maybe it's because there are still a significant number of organizations that haven't adopted it.

At the time I was introduced to Agile, I wasn't particularly enthusiastic about it. Waterfall may have its problems, but I was in an organization that didn't spend a significant amount of time writing design documents. My life as a developer generally consisted of being verbally given a set of features expected in the next release, being given a date when the next release was due, and being turned loose to make the magic happen. While this could certainly lead to the dreaded death march, it also gave me the freedom to structure my activities the way I wanted to. It also kept me free of the frequent scrutiny and accountability of a daily standup meeting where I would have to explain what I had worked on yesterday and what I would be working on today. If I decided to spend a week reinventing the wheel, I was free to do so without having that choice judged by anyone because they were blissfully unaware that I was doing it.

A former Director of Development under whom I worked used to refer to us as "code slingers." We just loved blasting away at our keyboards in the Wild West of software development. He was right. And to an extent, Agile practices represented the new sheriff in town that reigned in our maverick tendencies.

Agile had some work to do in winning me over.

It would be presumptuous to believe that Agile is the de-facto standard in software development houses or that all developers embrace it as something positive. Conversely, it would be naive to deny the significance of Agile in the world of software development. But what does that even mean? What, exactly, is its significance?

Ask the developers in an "Agile organization" what Agile is, and you'll likely get a very different answer than if you ask anyone beyond the level of a software development manager. Perhaps that is where this book has been the most enlightening.

Developers understand Agile to be a methodology for streamlining the development process and for making software development more predictable, more practicable, and more manageable. It's reasonable that we look at it from this perspective because it's the perspective that most directly affects us.

Speaking from personal experience, many developers are blissfully unaware of management's use of the metrics provided by the implementation of Agile practices and the data it produces. In some organizations, the entire development team participates in the meetings where these metrics are discussed; but in many others, the developers have no idea that these discussions even take place. Moreover, perhaps in some, those discussions don't actually happen.

While I have long been aware of this aspect of Agile, I still found it enlightening to understand the original intent and thought processes of the founders of this methodology that this book provides. It was also good to see those founders humanized. They weren't some set of ultra-elite software architects, ordained by the Software Engineering Masters or elected by the software programmer masses to hand down canon. They were a set of experienced developers with ideas about how to make their jobs, and their lives, easier and less stressful. They were tired of working in environments destined for failure and wanted to foster environments that allowed for success.

This sounds like most developers at every company where I've ever worked.

Had the Snowbird meeting taken place 15 years later, I could see it having been a number of developers with whom I have personally worked and myself, who convened that meeting and put those ideas to digital paper. But being just another group of seasoned developers, this group was prone to flights of fancy that might not play well in the real world of corporate software development. Maybe it all works as designed in the world of high-end consultants with the authority to make demands and hold organizations and management to their commitments, but most of us are grunts, cogs in the machinery of software factories. We are replaceable, and we have very little leverage. So when it comes to things like The Bill of Rights, we understand that this is an ideal, but one that is not realized for the majority of us.

With the social media communities of today, I am heartened to see many new developers extending themselves beyond the boundaries of a CS degree and 9-to-5 development job, connecting with other developers around the world, learning in any number of different ways, and putting their own knowledge and experiences out there to teach and inspire other fledgling developers. I fully expect the next sea change in methodology to emerge from a digital gathering of these young up-and-comers.

So while we await the Next Big Thing that the next generation will reveal to us, let's take a minute to reassess where we are and what we have to work with at present.

Now that you've read this book, contemplate it for a minute. Consider the aspects of Agile you may have known about but to which you hadn't given much thought. Think about it from the perspective of the business analyst, project manager, or anything-other-than-dev manager responsible for planning releases or creating product roadmaps. Consider what value the input from developers into the Agile processes brings to them. Understand how your input into the process affects more than just your workload for the next two weeks. Then go back and skim the book again. If you approach it with this broader perspective in mind, I believe you will glean even more useful insights.

Once you've done that, encourage another developer in your organization to read it and undergo the same introspection. Maybe even hand the book to someone who, wait for it... isn't a developer. Give it to someone on the "business" side of the company. I would almost guarantee you that The Bill of Rights is something they have never given much thought to. Your life stands to be much more pleasant if you get them to understand that these rights are just as integral to Agile as the metrics that they pull out of it.

You might say that Agile has become something akin to a religion in the realm of software development. Many of us have accepted it as a best practice. Why? For many, it's because they've been told so. It has become tradition; it's just how things are done. For a new generation of corporate developers, it just is. They, and even many of us old-timers don't really know where it all came from, nor what the original goals, purposes, and practices were all about. Say what you will about religion, but the best adherents to it are those who make the effort to understand what they believe, beyond just believing what they are told. And as with religion, there isn't one universally accepted, one-size-fits-all version.

Imagine the significance of having a view into the origins of your religion, an understanding of the events and thoughts that shaped what would become canon for you. When it comes to your professional life, that's exactly what you have here. Use it for all it's worth, evangelize it to the others in your sphere of influence, and reclaim the original goal, the goal you and practically everyone you've ever worked with have longed for, talked about, and probably given up on. Make successful software development achievable. Make organizational goals attainable. Make the process of making things better.

INDEX